THE HANDBAG

THE HANDBAG

AN ILLUSTRATED HISTORY

CAROLINE COX

COLLINS|DESIGN

An Imprint of HarperCollinsPublishers

To Lionel and Neil

Thanks to Sheila Ableman, Edward Darley, Leona Curran and all my friends at Vidal Sassoon, Karen Ings, Maggie Norden, Marnie Fogg, Alex Marsden, Abigail Healey, Ann Carter, Anne McDowall, Isobel Gillan, and Nikki Lloyd.

The Handbag: An Illustrated History
Copyright © 2007 by Caroline Cox

HarperCollins books may be purchased for educational, business, or sales promotional use. For information, please write: Special Markets Department, HarperCollins Publishers, 10 East 53rd Street, New York, NY 10022.

First Edition
First published in the United States and Canada in 2007 by:
Collins Design
An Imprint of HarperCollins*Publishers*
10 East 53rd Street
New York, NY 10022
Tel: (212) 207-7000
Fax: (212) 207-7654
collinsdesign@harpercollins.com
www.harpercollins.com

First published in the United Kingdom in 2007 by:
Aurum Press Limited
7 Greenland Street, London NW1 0ND
www.aurumpress.co.uk

Distributed throughout the United States and Canada by:
HarperCollins*Publishers*
10 East 53rd Street
New York, NY 10022
Fax: (212) 207-7654

Library of Congress Control Number: 2007923537

ISBN: 978-0-06-122738-7
ISBN-10: 0-06-122738-2

Printed in China
First printing, 2007

CONTENTS

LEFT *The twenties flapper was a new modern woman, a fashion consumer par excellence, who was willing to buy an array of handbags in bright modernist designs and new materials.*

RIGHT *Fifties chic and understated elegance changed the look of handbags. Fashionable women craved discreet styles in luxurious crocodile, kid, or snakeskin.*

earners and thus economically in control. It was not until the end of the nineteenth century that a woman needed a more substantial handbag to carry items of daily use.

With the expansion of the railway network and the increased participation of middle- and upper-class women in travel as a leisure activity, bags became more and more important. Liberated from the shackles of the home and hearth, no longer content solely with matters wholly domestic, women became increasingly vocal about their rights and, bizarrely or not, bags were at the forefront of debate. Women argued for the right to bear pockets rather than sport tiny bags, and in 1915, Charlotte Perkins Gilman imagined a feminist utopia where this was so in *Herland*.

By the 1920s, bags were needed for shopping and cosmetics—now freely available and freely worn, no longer the preserve only of the "working girl"—

and the most daring of flappers carried bags with special compartments for lipstick and powder and mirrors in which to paint their faces. This was the era when the handbag, fashioned out of all manner of exotic materials and embellished with sequins, crystals, "liquid" metal mesh, and marabou trim, really came into its own. The new streamlined shape of the clutch bag reflected the modernity of art deco, as did the use of Perspex and Bakelite. Meanwhile, Roman couturière Elsa Schiaparelli collaborated with surrealist maverick Salvador Dalí to conceive fantastic designs in the shape of flower pots, bird cages, and apples of bright red suede.

During the following decade, Hollywood introduced a generation of women to the notion of high glamour, exquisitely expressed in images of film star Jean Harlow swathed in white mink posed with a Swarovski crystal-encrusted satin bag. This was also the decade in which the first leather shoulder bags were designed, although they really caught on in Paris during the Nazi occupation of 1940–4. The shoulder bag was functional for urban life, practical for women cycling around the city streets.

Sophisticated and fashionable women in the 1950s wanted to express a different femininity to that of the austere war years—a femininity that was glamorous and chic rather than utilitarian. Designs informed by fanciful romance rather than "make do and mend" fitted the bill. The elegant alligator clutch with a *griffe*, or designer label, was one such bag; held under one arm rather than shrugged across the shoulder, this was a smart bag for tripping around town in stilettos rather than striding around a bomb site.

This was also the era in which some of the most ubiquitous designer handbags were created—Coco Chanel's black quilted-leather bag with gilt-chain handle in 1955 and Gucci's bamboo-handled bag in 1957, to name but two—and the time that celebrity bag endorsement began. Grace Kelly was snapped by paparazzi attempting to conceal her pregnancy with

her Hermès Kelly bag in 1956; the Kelly went on to become a global best seller and remains one today, half a century later.

The space race had a huge influence on sixties design, with inflatable furniture, monochromatic paintings, and pop art hues. The fine tailoring and craftsmanship of the 1950s was discarded in favor of free-form, unstructured bags in abstract shapes and artificial fibers. Paco Rabanne created his metal mesh mini-dresses with matching shoulder bags, and no self-respecting modette would be without her white plastic purse. By the end of the decade, the global protests of the hippie movement and its symbolic identification with poverty expressed itself sartorially in the casual tote bag, customized for individuality, and the satchel or duffle bag. Bags, once merely utilitarian, had become props of anti-fashion rebellion. This anti-fashion aesthetic continued into the 1970s, as bags took on serious satchel shapes in keeping with the no-frills ethos of feminism. It would take disco to lighten up the bag and punk to add a dash of forbidden fetishism.

Handbags in the 1980s were as brash as the decade itself, icons of conspicuous consumption when the ethos of "greed is good" predominated in the global city. This was the era of look-at-me logos, branding, and designer suits. In her new persona as executive dominatrix, the power-dressed woman stalked her way through the workplace with a bag to match her Armani suiting. Enter the status bag, handcrafted out of luxury material, evoking the designer classic of the 1950s. Margaret Thatcher's black leather Ferragamo became an evocative symbol of Conservatism; according to popular mythology, it was also a weapon she used to quell her political enemies. The verb "handbagging" has since entered into common parlance.

By the 1990s and 2000s, the designer bag had triumphed with the invention of instant classics such as the Fendi Baguette, the Lady Dior, and the much-copied Vuitton Graffiti. Luxurious objects such as these have made the bag the most fashionable of accessories, the one designer item many women are prepared to invest in, and the last acceptable bearer of an atelier's monogram. The designer handbag is no longer the preserve of the elite or those with celebrity status. And there is a magical reason for this: Unlike designer clothes, with handbags, one size fits all, and the ownership of the most fashionable is not precluded by anybody's race, age, social status, or weight—only by the health of their personal credit.

In the first decade of the twenty-first century, handbags, these markers of mobility, have never been more important—or more enormous—as they must accommodate all the paraphernalia a modern woman needs. Now it's Blackberries, hair straighteners, and cell phones, as well as purse, cosmetics, and chewing gum. The must-have bag of the season may be a lusted-after designer item that can make or break a fashion name. But bags are more than just a logo; they are an intimate part of the body's silhouette, survival kits for life in the urban jungle, and at the same time an indicator of fashionability.

ONE

THE BIRTH OF THE BAG

Lucy Locket lost her pocket
Kitty Fisher found it
Not a penny was there in it
Only ribbons round it.

ANON

LEFT *Pouches were the precursor of the bag*
and hung from a girdle at the waist. The
size of the purse indicated wealth—a tiny
purse suggested others were employed to
do more onerous carrying.

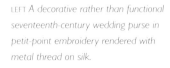

The handbag is a truly modern phenomenon: A bewitching accessory that has the ability to shift its shape with every nuance of fashion. It can be functional or fanciful, but its appearance is inextricably bound to changes in the fashionable silhouette, a symbiotic relationship that began in the early nineteenth century and continues today. Certain rules apply: The voluminous skirt, for instance, makes handbags rather superfluous, as anything bulky can be hidden away among its luxurious folds in intimate and secretive pockets—as was the case in the 1860s, when the vogue for the expansive crinoline skirt was at its height. As fashions became more body conscious in the early twentieth century, so bags came to the fore, *objets de luxe* that continue to play a key role in modish display.

Before the birth of the bag, items of personal use were transported in androgynous cloth or leather pouches that dangled from the waist—the Ancient Greek *byrasa*, for instance, or the Roman *bursa*. The smaller the pouch, the higher the social status; nonchalantly sporting a tiny bag suggested that there were others of a lowlier status employed to do all the more burdensome lifting.

Smaller handheld purses were also in use from the medieval period onward, but as decorative items of symbolic significance rather than objects of everyday use. The *almoner*, for instance, was, in the words of bag historian Anna Johnson, "a showy coin purse designed to draw attention to public display of largesse" when coins were given out ceremonially by noblemen to the poor.[1]

The wedding purse, usually presented as a gift to a happy couple on the day of the nuptials, was another example of an object of ritual rather than function. In many ancient cultures, the purse symbolized a womb, which in order to be filled had to be fertilized with seeds. The Roman goddess of fertility, Uberitas, provides an early example: She is

often depicted holding both a cornucopia and a purse.
Uberitas links a plentiful harvest with its source, the
woman's womb or purse, and this symbolism filtered
into early pagan wedding rituals. At first the purse
was filled with money "harvested" from the wedding
guests, but by the eighteenth century it was carried
by a bride bedecked in orange blossom. Orange
blossom bouquets or wreaths were significant:
Because of the plant's rare ability to bloom and bear
fruit at the same time, they were seen as Mediterranean
tokens of fruitfulness. The fashion spread across
Europe after the Crusades into Spain, France, and
eventually England, most famously at the wedding of
Queen Victoria and Prince Albert. Juxtaposing the
purse–womb with such a fecund plant bestowed a
symbol of fertility upon the bride and groom.

By the sixteenth century, pouches could be
purely functional or, for those of wealth and social
status, richly embellished and finely wrought from
cloth of silver or gold embroidered with silver–gilt
thread and dotted with seed pearls. When dangling
from a girdle, pouches such as these presented a

tempting target for thieves or cutpurses, who used
cuttle knives to slice through the base. One
unsuspecting victim knew nothing "till he had sold a
peck of meal, and offered for to change money, and
then he found his purse bottomless."[2]

As a precautionary measure, the pouch and the
purse began to be hidden about the person, in
women's muffs or in the folds of shirts and skirts, and
by the seventeenth century, pockets had taken over
from pouches in both male and female dress. A
woman's pockets were a little different from a man's,
however, not an intrinsic part of a garment but
individual pouches wrought of linen worn on a band
at the waist under the skirt and next to the skin. Many
were delicately embroidered in silk and held items
such as the pocket handkerchief and pocket book.

Pockets were intimate, classed almost as items of
underwear—secret places hidden under a skirt's
sumptuous lengths of material and reached by a slit in
the skirt. It didn't take much imagination to make
connections with other intimate "pockets" about the
person. With all these saucy connotations, the thieving
of a pocket was all the more risqué an act, as a light-
fingered pickpocket was touching an incredibly
intimate item. One pickpocket boasted in 1751: "My
chief dexterity was in robbing the ladies. There is a
peculiar delicacy required in whipping one's hand up
a lady's petticoats and carrying off her pockets."[3]

When the pocket evolved into the handbag—
essentially a handle was added to a pocket—these
rather risqué connotations were retained. The
connection was clear as a reporter on the *Imperial
Weekly Gazette* realized, writing in 1804: "While men
have their hands in their pockets so grand, ladies have
pockets to wear in the hand."[4]

These prototype handbags were given the name
reticule, derived from the Latin word *rete* meaning net.
(Net pouches used to carry belongings in Ancient
Rome were called *reticulum.*) By the seventeenth
century the word *reticle* entered the English language
as the name for a little net used to fish in streams and

LEFT *In a 1799 fashion plate from* Costumes Parisien, *a fashionable lady carries an embroidered hexagonally shaped reticule that contrasts with her simple neoclassical muslin gown.*

RIGHT *By the early nineteenth century, the reticule had become a fashionable accessory for European women. This 1830s English example is of ivory silk embroidered with a bouquet of flowers and has chenille tassels.*

rock pools—a name perfectly suited to the small pockets or pouch-shaped bags sported by women of fashion in the early nineteenth century, hence the name *reticule*. These early handbags were also daring, one of the first examples of underwear as outerwear—and thus for many a rather absurd affectation. The idea of a woman parading her personal belongings in a visible pocket was an act akin to lifting up her skirts and publicly revealing her underwear. For many observers, the easy conversion of "reticule" into "ridicule" was irresistible—the reticule was clearly ridiculous.

The fashion for the ridiculous reticule was also linked to the fad for the neoclassical style in Europe. After the French Revolution, a mania for all things Greek and Roman developed, spurred on by the notion that these ancient Mediterranean cultures were examples of utopian democracy. To differentiate themselves from members of the French court, whose rather overblown garb had been characterized by wigs, peach satin, and high heels—a look that in a newly democratic France reeked of aristocratic debauchery—women of fashion began to dress down.

Draped muslin worn empire-line to create a tubular, languid silhouette became de rigueur in the fashionable salons of Europe, the muslin sometimes dampened to further reveal the delights of the body beneath and, of course, potentially the outline of a lady's pockets. Footman William Taylor wrote in his diary of young ladies "naked to the waist, only just a little bit of dress hanging on the shoulder, the breasts are quite exposed except a little bit to hide the nipples. Plenty of false hair and teeth and paint."[5] Meanwhile, another contemporary wrote in 1794 of his shock at seeing women at a public ball in Paris showing "bare arms, naked breasts, feet shod with sandals, hair turned in tresses around their heads by modish hairdressers, who study the antique busts. Guess where are the pockets of these dancers? They have none; they stick their fan in their belt, and

lodge in their bosom a slight purse of morocco leather in which there are a few spare guineas."[6]

It was this sexy diaphanous look of the late eighteenth century that led directly to the development of the reticule, or indispensable as it was known in England, created to combat a 1790s version of the visible panty line—the visible pocket line. The new indispensable, so-called because it carried all things considered crucial to the fashionable woman about town, took over from the pocket and evolved into an exquisitely embroidered bag fashioned out of the most sumptuous damask, satin, and velvet. As bag historian Claire Wilcox describes, the reticule could take many shapes, but hexagonal or lozenge shapes were the most popular as "their flat sides provided a vehicle for embroidered, painted and applied decoration, which often featured various Neoclassical, architectural and floral motifs. Some were soft, others had round, stiffened bases, while further variants were based on novelties, such as pineapple-shaped reticules worked in silk crochet."[7]

In her reticule or indispensable, a woman transported her most essential items for life in modern

BELOW A 1800 caricature by James Gillray
makes a clear link between the bag and a
lady's more intimate parts. Here a man
searches for a lady's "indispensible,"
attempting to find it under her skirts.

The MAN of FEELING, in search of INDISPENSIBLES; — a Scene at the little
umber of disputes having arisen in the Beau Monde, respecting the Exact Situation of the Ladies Indispensibles (or new Invented Pockets,) w
more eligible situation, the above Search took place, in order to determine precisely the Longitude of those inestimable conveniences.

Europe: Her rouge, powder, fan, perfume, and *cartes de visite*. The reticule was also for display—much as a Balenciaga bag is today—its very sumptuousness hinting at the fortunes of the family, while at the same time its contents remained completely hidden. Thus, this forerunner of the handbag was a paradox, simultaneously revealing yet concealing, outwardly displayed yet still mysteriously intimate.

One's character being revealed "accidentally" through the appearance of one's bag fuels the narrative of *The Reticule* (1850), a moral tale of mid-nineteenth-century femininity set in Virginia. The story features a Miss Nancy Craig, a gentlewoman and spinster of reduced circumstances, who regularly gathered with other ladies of Williamsburg for a dish of tea and a gossip:

> … *her straightened means made her relish the tea and cakes as much as the gossip. She realized, poor lady! the bareness of her own larder at home and was glad not only to enjoy the hospitality offered at the time, but to reinforce her frugal store by any titbit which could be secretly carried home. The secret was an open one, Miss Nancy carried with her a roomy reticule and its increasing weight and girth coupled with the disappearance of muffins and cakes, or fragments of loaf-sugar, was the source of much sly amusement among her hostesses.*
>
> *At one party young Mr. Alexander Southall undertook to be witty at her expense, and pretending a curiosity as to the use made of the fashionable reticules or pockets carried by the ladies, declared his intention of examining them all, vowing that the dame or damsel who refused to exhibit the contents of her bag, should pay him the forfeit of a kiss.*
>
> *The examination proceeded merrily, until he reached Miss Nancy who exclaimed cheerfully and without embarrassment, "Law, Alex, I'd just as soon kiss you as not!"*[8]

A contemporary post-Freudian reading of Miss Nancy's "roomy reticule" could make an obvious

analogy between the "old bag" and its owner, but this modern interpretation was one that was also made at the time. The use of the term *purse* for the female pudenda dates back as far as the early seventeenth century, and the insult *old bag* became popular in the mid- to late-1800s to describe a rather unattractive woman no longer in the bloom of youth. It is an association common to many languages, and one commented upon by writer Alison Lurie in her definitive study of the semiotics of dress, *The Language of Clothes*. Lurie sees the bag as "the most universally recognized sexual indicator in women," and the examination of Miss Nancy's "reticule" by a much younger man has rather scandalous connotations as a result.[9] Her willingness to accept a kiss rather than Alexander's more intimate explorations is quite understandable.

A rather more dramatic example of the reticule's relationship with female sexuality appears in Leo Tolstoy's *Anna Karenina* of 1875. In the novel's powerful denouement, Anna throws her little red velvet handbag onto the railway track before committing suicide following her tortured love affair with young officer Aleksey Vronsky.

> *She tried to fling herself below the wheels of the first carriage as it reached her; but the red bag which she tried to drop out of her hand delayed her, and she was too late; she missed the moment. She had to wait for the next carriage … And exactly at the moment when the space between the wheels came opposite her, she dropped the red bag, and drawing her head back into her shoulders, fell on her hands under the carriage.*[10]

Her red bag, the color of her illicit passion and an emblem of her own sex, causes her problems to the end.

The reticule, although pretty, was by no means universally popular, and by the mid-nineteenth century, women were beginning to realize that men had a distinct advantage over them when it came to

LEFT *A French woman at the end of the Napoleonic wars in 1813 holds a lozenge-shaped reticule—a necessity because a pocket full of objects would show through the draped material of her skirts.*

BELOW RIGHT *Madame Recamier was a leading figure in the literary and political circles of late eighteenth-century Paris. Her finely embroidered silk purse would have been the height of French fashion.*

carrying things around. In describing her mode of dress in the 1860s, novelist Alison Uttley wrote of this disparity, comparing her own lone reticule to her father's clothes:

> *He had many pockets in the large loosely fitting coat, and the waistcoat, too, had odd extra pockets for secret things. These pockets were a source of wonder to me, for he put his hand in one and then another, bringing out strange things, especially after he had driven to the town. Out would come sausages, sweets, cartridges, a toy trumpet, a doll, a musical box, a bottle of liniment, a box of pills, a new pair of spectacles, a bag of rosy pears, more and more things, till one stared as if he were a conjuror, and my mother protested that he would spoil the shape of his coat. "What are pockets for if you can't fill them?" he would ask, and I wished I had more than my solitary pocket, which hung at that time like Lucy Locket's, dangling from my waistband, a gathered bag.[11]*

The bag was a gendered object and was a clear example of how the differences in the fashionable attire of men and that of women were becoming ever more apparent as the nineteenth century progressed. Men and women were inhabiting increasingly separate spheres, both physically and aesthetically, with women's realm being the home and hearth and men's the world of work. As design historian Penny Sparke puts it, "within the feminine sphere objects became, first and foremost, symbols, sacrificing their utilitarian features to their symbolic functions."[12]

Fashion reflected these symbolic notions. A husband had to look sober and respectable, as befitted a gentleman of industry who worked outside of the home for the good of his family. A woman, meanwhile, was to stay at home and look after domestic affairs and the children, but at the same time she had to appear as an object of sweetly feminine decoration. The fashionable facade of the "angel in the house" was firstly a pleasure for her husband to see after a hard day's toil at the office, but also established to his peers the man's own credit-worthiness and acumen in the financial world. As Leonore Davidoff and Catherine Hall write in their historical survey of this period:

> *The contrast between the straight lines, practical materials and businesslike images of men's clothes and the soft, flowing curved lines, the rich colours and textures, elaborate detail and constricting shape of women's clothes was becoming a powerful part of gendered segregation … Ruggedness of features, a certain disdain for appearances, even brusqueness, were signs of manliness … The diametrically opposite feminine ideal was symbolized by the wood anemone or rosebud.[13]*

Women were part of nature, fragile, pliable, and decorative like flowers, and their appearance was supposed to suggest these qualities above others of a more practical nature—those were the preserve of the lower classes. Gowns were decorated with floral motifs, hats were bedecked with artificial blooms, and reticules bore patterns of roses, birds, buttercups, and daisies intricately worked with Bohemian glass beads, Berlin wool-work, or knitted silk.

(2294)

LEFT *A fashion plate of 1825 shows a woman dressed in a blue-gray redingote holding a whimsical reticule in the shape of an iced dessert in a dish.*

BELOW RIGHT *The carpet bag was a sturdy container for the male or female traveler and was of made of lengths of wool carpeting. This colorful example, secured with a metal lock, dates from the 1840s.*

The fashionable woman was too delicate to carry anything of consequence except a few "dainty props," a notion that still has resonance today, as feminist writer Susan Brownmiller writes: "Romantically the feminine ideal is often pictured with something pretty and fragile to occupy the hands; a nosegay of violets, the bridal bouquet of white stephanotis and orange blossoms, a sheaf of long-stemmed roses presented to the prima ballerina as she takes her curtain call amidst applause."[14]

The reticule was just such a dainty prop. Like the parasol or fan, it played its part in the Victorian construction of womanhood—it was decorative, impractical (as it couldn't really carry very much), and it, in turn, prevented a woman from carrying anything else. The mid-century fashion for slope-shouldered gowns and shawls—which prevented the arms from being raised to any great degree—along with the poke bonnet—which limited sight—and the sundry ribbons, ringlets, boned stays, and full skirts that women had to endure, discouraged them from doing anything remotely physical. As Davidoff and Hall suggest, "their style was a deliberate foil to the new masculine archetype."[15] This style had class connotations too, of course: It was for the woman who could afford not to work and who had a man to provide for her. For the working woman, life was a little different, as her uniform of plain black gown, laden wicker basket, and armfuls of packages suggested.

The fashion for the reticule waned a little in direct proportion to the widening of women's skirts, in particular the exaggerated proportions of the crinoline, which allowed women's pockets to reappear in the 1860s. They continued to be used right up to 1892, when Lady Viola Greville, a renowned writer on ladies' etiquette, complained of "The average woman [who] still carries her purse in her hand, and dives into the recesses of an impossible receptacle, situated somewhere in the back breadths of her gown, for her pocket-handkerchief, her letters, her notebook, her card-case, or her money – the whole forming a disagreeably hard aggregation on which she patiently effects to sit."[16]

A more enduring bag revolution was to come, predicated on notions of women and their physical mobility rather than mere changes in skirt shape. It was in this pivotal era that the whole notion of travel and exploration for both men and women developed with the growth of the railway network, the introduction of transatlantic crossings by Cunard, and the expansion of the British Empire. The vogue for the voyage fueled the desire for fashionable luggage such as suitcases, dressing cases with silver-topped bottles and manicure sets, hat and shoeboxes—out of which the true handbag developed. The carpet bag, for instance, enjoyed a huge surge in popularity in the 1870s due to its combination of portability and roominess, obviating the need for the heavy trunk on short journeys by road or rail. Although we now associate the carpet bag with women—particularly Mary Poppins, whose cavernous carpet bag held the contents of a small apartment, including a large gilded mirror, an aspidistra plant, and a hat stand—it was originally a man's bag. Phineas Fogg, for

RIGHT *The Louis Vuitton brand was the height of luxury in the nineteenth century. Here, the luggage of an Irish landowner includes a leather hatbox, Gladstone bag, and a large Vuitton case.*

instance, one of fiction's most famed travelers, used one as this passage from Jules Verne's *Around the World in Eighty Days* (1873) reveals:

> *"Around the world," murmured Passepartout.*
> *"In eighty days," replied Mr Fogg. "So we haven't a moment to lose."*
> *"But the trunks?" gasped Passepartout, unconsciously swaying his head from right to left.*
> *"We'll have no trunks. Just a carpet bag. Inside, two woollen shirts, three pairs of stockings. The same for you. We'll buy along the way."* [17]

Carpet bags were tough and sturdy, made out of scraps of carpet rolled and fastened at the edges and, as the *Scientific American Supplement* wrote in 1886, "still unsurpassed by any, where rough wear is the principal thing to be studied. Such a bag, if constructed of good Brussels carpeting and unquestionable workmanship, will last a lifetime." [18] Robert Louis Stevenson lauded the hard-wearing qualities of his carpet bag, the perfect accompaniment to the lone intrepid traveler, in *Travels with a Donkey in the Cevennes*, published in 1870. For him, as for many, the carpet bag doubled as a blanket when the sides were unhitched, and his "railway rug, which being also in the form of a bag, made me a double castle for cold nights." [19]

The carpet bag was certainly functional, but what about elegance and luxury, key cornerstones of fashion and dandified display? Step forward Louis Vuitton, the creator of the designer bag. Vuitton, a name now synonymous with luxury leather goods, was originally employed as a box maker and luggage packer for Paris' haute bourgeoisie, a job in which he reached the giddy heights of packing gowns for the Empress Eugenie, consort of Napoleon III.

Traveling by coach in the mid-nineteenth century was an uncomfortable experience. Journeys were long and roads rutted and potholed, which meant that any precious objects had to be packed carefully to survive the rigors of travel. Thus it became customary for all items of value to be

LEFT *At the London sales of 1908, female shoppers can be clearly seen carrying an array of small handbags. Women had become more socially mobile and needed the handbag to transport their daily needs while they were away from home.*

BELOW *Suffragettes were vociferous in their demand for equal rights with men—and equally adamant about the need for substantial pockets rather than tiny bags.*

SUFFRAGETTE SERIES Nº 12.

OFFICIAL BALLoT

I LOVE MY HUSBAND, BUT—
OH YOU VOTE

COPYRIGHTED

1909 BY DUNSTON-WEILER LITHOGRAPH CO.

transported in made-to-measure wooden boxes that could withstand the journey and the notoriously rough touch of French baggage handlers.

Vuitton's reputation as the trusted box maker and packer of the Empress's possessions led him to open his own store in 1854, the Maison Louis Vuitton. It was here that he invented the first flat trunk, an elegant, streamlined departure from the old-style rustic trunk. The latter had a domed lid to allow rainwater to drain off and was made of pigskin complete with bristles, the sight of which, as French historian Paul-Gerard Pasols comments, "must have given travellers a sense, not of the pleasures before them, but of cold, uncertainty, pitfalls to overcome, maybe even packs of wolves to fight off."[20]

Vuitton's trunk was different: Flat, elegant, and light, fashioned out of waterproofed gray canvas with a trim of lacquered iron, it was ingeniously stackable—a key example of early modernist design. With the creation of this simple yet innovative object, Louis Vuitton had managed to make a crucial link between modernity, luxury, and travel. The company capitalized upon this for more than a hundred years, cleverly making the brand highly visible on the exterior with the introduction of the Monogram canvas in 1896. This was the canvas used to make one of the world's most exquisite and sought-after handbags, the Noe, designed in 1931 for carrying five bottles of Champagne.

With increased possibilities for travel, women also needed a more substantial handbag to carry their items for daily use. As women became a more tangible presence on the city streets, so did their bags, which changed from dainty reticules into shapes that were sturdier and more substantial. No longer content to stay at home, increasingly vocal about their rights, and wanting to visit the new cathedrals of consumption— the department stores—to spend money, women needed a way of transporting more possessions so that they could stay out longer. A handbag was a necessity for a woman who wanted to browse the windows of

Macy's in New York City or the stores of the Champs-Elysées in Paris or London's Regent Street, to parade along the glittering facades of the new shopping arcades, to take afternoon tea at one of the best hotels, or to enjoy a theatrical matinee. As cultural historian Elizabeth Wilson comments:

In a very real way the department store assisted the freeing of middle-class women from the shackles of the home. It became a place where women could meet their women friends in safety and comfort, unchaperoned, and to which they could repair for refreshment and rest…. Shopping was a social event. Advances in architecture opened up fresh possibilities in London when the new Regent Street was designed by Nash with an elegant colonnade. It became the mecca of the fashionable shopper, the thoroughfare was a promenade, and society's elite went there at least as much to see and be seen as to shop.[21]

For the first time, a woman was in charge of her own purse strings rather than at the beck and call of her husband, and handbags reflected this shift in domestic economics. Early examples were quite functional objects derived from men's handheld luggage bags, all leather with locks, keys, and

compartments. The first bags to be actually called *hand-bags* appeared in the first decade of the twentieth century. Edwardian handbags were essentially miniature suitcases with lots of internal compartments, to stress the utilitarian, masculine nature of their origins and to mark them out from the reticule, which spoke of feminine frippery rather than woman as an intrepid traveler. A key change was the handle, giving women a sturdy grip on their belongings, whereas the reticule dangled loosely from the wrist. And there were other important differences, as Anna Johnson comments:

Unlike a flimsy mesh reticule or a decorative coin purse sealed by a string, this bag snapped shut, and for the first time women could carry their things with some degree of privacy. Men, who had long carried a lady's fan or her money, were supplanted by increasingly practical, brilliantly structured bags, and they have been mystified and excluded by the handbag ever since.[22]

These early leather handbags were not designed as such but created by leather goods companies such as Vuitton, Gucci (est. 1906), and Prada (est. 1913), companies that had originally sold utilitarian objects such as harnesses, saddles, and luggage—the couture bag was yet to come. Hermès was just such a company. Founded in 1837 by Thierry Hermès, the company originally specialized in saddlery—finely wrought bridles and harnesses for the carriage trade—and by the 1870s was supplying all the royal courts of Europe from their premises on the rue Faubourg Saint-Honoré in Paris. As the century progressed and the horse began to be overtaken by more modern forms of transportation, the company realized it had to adapt or die. The resulting trunks, bags, and overnight cases consolidated the company's reputation as the purveyor of beautifully handcrafted luggage. Using the most exquisite leathers, including alligator, ostrich, and crocodile, while retaining attention to detail and durability, Hermès transitioned from making utilitarian nose bags and saddle bags to creating stylish

PIERRE SOUVESTRE & MARCEL ALLAIN

FANTÔMAS

L'AGENT SECRET

LE VOLUME COMPLET
65
CENTIMES

FAYARD ÉDITEUR DU "LIVRE POPULAIRE" PARIS

BURKHARDT & CIE., PFORZHEIM.

handbags for the new female consumer. The luxury branded handbag as we know it was born.

Not all Edwardian women were happy with the handbag, however. In particular, American feminists were appalled at the death of women's pockets at the expense of the handheld bag. Leather handbags, which were increasingly regarded as wholly feminine objects as the new century progressed, were, they believed, physically restrictive, and because of their meager dimensions could never be as functional as men's pockets. Women such as Alice Duer Miller and Charlotte Perkins Gilman seized on men's pockets versus women's bags as a metaphor for sexual inequality and the struggle for social rights, and fashionable accessories became the focus of impassioned protest in much the same way as the bra did in the late 1960s. In *Herland*, for instance, written by Perkins Gilman in 1915, an Amazonian utopia is imagined in which "women had pockets in surprising number and variety. They were in all their garments, and one in particular was shingled with them."[23] And in the same author's *If I were a Man* (1914), heroine Molly magically changes sex. As a man, her pockets:

> … *came as a revelation. Of course she had known they were there, had counted them, made fun of them, mended them, even envied them; but she never had dreamed of how it felt to have pockets.*
>
> *Behind her newspaper she let her consciousness, that odd mingled consciousness, rove from pocket to pocket, realizing the armored assurance of having all those things at hand, instantly get-at-able, ready to meet emergencies. The cigar case gave her a warm feeling of comfort—it was full; the firmly held fountain pen, safe unless she stood on her head; the keys, pencils, letters, documents, notebook, check book, bill folder—all at once, with a deep rushing sense of power and pride, she felt what she had never felt before in all her life—the possession of money, of her own earned money—hers to give or to withhold, not to beg for, tease for, wheedle for—hers.[24]*

I found this elf perched on a tree
An caught him quick to send to thee!

Alice Duer Miller, a feminist and journalist who wrote a popular column for the *New York Tribune* entitled "Are Women People?" satirized the use of pockets in 1915 in an article with the headline "Why We Oppose Pockets for Women!" It ran:

1. *Because pockets are not a natural right.*
2. *Because the great majority of women do not want pockets. If they did they would have them.*
3. *Because whenever women have had pockets they have not used them.*
4. *Because women are required to carry enough things as it is, without the additional burden of pockets.*
5. *Because it would make dissension between husband and wife as to whose pockets were to be filled.*
6. *Because it would destroy man's chivalry toward woman, if he did not have to carry all her things in his pockets.*
7. *Because men are men, and women are women. We must not fly in the face of nature.*
8. *Because pockets have been used by men to carry tobacco, pipes, whiskey flasks, chewing gum and compromising letters. We see no reason to suppose that women would use them more wisely.[25]*

Many women loved the new handbag, not realizing that it represented for early feminists "life in a

gilded cage." These were perhaps the sort of women who, according to Loelia, Duchess of Westminster,

> *… liked a world where mashers treated every female as though she were a dream of beauty, where gentlemen did not swear in front of ladies, and where husbands really did shield their wives from the unpleasant side of life. If they were lucky they could go from the cradle to the grave just writing letters and cheques, giving orders to the servants and never bothering about anything so sordid as "business", or setting foot in a bank or an office of any kind, or having the faintest idea what their men folk were talking about when they were not there.[26]*

These women were prepared to wear the new hobble skirt with its tortuously slim lines that made pockets impossible and a bag renaissance inevitable. Indeed, many handbag forms appeared in the early twentieth century: The Dorothy bag, an Edwardian version of the reticule with its drawstring top and soft material; small purses with wrist straps; the opera bag to hold telescopic opera glasses, a program, and a fan; and the mesh bag, which enjoyed a vogue that lasted well into the 1930s.

The company most associated with the design and development of the mesh bag is Whiting and Davies, founded in 1876 and still in business today. The American company produced its first mesh bag in 1892 and by the 1920s was producing bags for top couturiers Paul Poiret and Elsa Schiaparelli. A typical Whiting and Davies mesh bag was constructed of silver or base metal rings intricately linked together into a fine mesh, which appears to be a derivation of chain mail, as used in medieval armor. Appearing at the time of the increasing vocalization of women's rights in America and the suffragette movement in England, the essentially masculine, military look of the mesh bag is interesting. The mesh bag appears decorative yet is protective and hard to penetrate, subtly suggesting being on guard against intruders.

The military connotations of the mesh bag seem to undermine the bag as dainty prop. Perhaps as a

result of its aggressive connotations, the chain mail was offset by an aesthetic "softening" in the 1920s, when new screen-printing techniques were introduced, allowing the mesh to be covered in more traditionally feminine motifs of flowers and fruit. Women were being put firmly back in their place at the center of nature rather than of culture.

Many mesh bags were also tiny, because middle-class women, in particular, still didn't carry that much around—they didn't need house keys as a servant would always be around to open up, and a large amount of money was unnecessary as most families had accounts at their local stores. A woman of fashion needed only her visiting cards, a small powder puff, a change purse, and a vial of smelling salts.

Cecil Beaton remembered "ladies of the middle classes … in hansom carriages as they paid afternoon calls. Their white kid gloves were of immaculate quality. Over one wrist they carried a small, square gold mesh bag containing a gold pencil, a handkerchief, and a flat gold wallet which held their calling cards."[27] The miniature mesh bag carried by Beaton's Belle Epoque ladies also suggested, of course, that any large packages would be carried by a man, be he servant, porter, or husband. A wealthy woman didn't need to be weighed down by anything superfluous.

The Edwardian lady of leisure used her bag for her discreet amours rather than anything more practical. The famed couturier Lucile, who designed delicious gowns of rose pink chiffon and lavender lace in the 1910s, recalled an occasion when

One day a woman came in to choose a dress. She was very beautiful, and married to a rich man. Everybody supposed the marriage to be ideally happy. She began to talk to me, and I could see that she was amused at something.

She said; "I have just come back from abroad, and soon I am going to enjoy myself very much indeed."

I asked her what she was going to do, and she replied that it was something she had already done

several times, and the doing of it had given her the greatest thrill of her life.

She explained that her husband, who was very much in love with her, was very strict, and was above all things madly jealous. She used to slip away abroad on some pretext or other, and there indulge in a passionate love affair with some man whose appearance pleased her. She would then arrange that the lover of the moment should write to her the most devoted letters. These she would keep carefully. On her return to England she would invite her husband's and her own relations to a dull family dinner. On some occasions she used to place herself next to her husband. Then she would deliberately lay her bag between them, close to his hand. In the bag reposed her lover's letters, any one of which would have been sufficient to wreck her marriage and condemn her to a life of social ostracism. It was a marvellous thrill, she confessed to me, with shining eyes.

"Why once," she said, "he actually took up the bag and examined the clasp. I thought he was going to examine it. It was the most exciting moment I have ever had in my life!"[28]

The idea of a woman as an *objet de luxe* was to change, however, as more women began to leave the comforts of home for the world of work, particularly after the First World War. Households were getting smaller and domestic servants were increasingly unnecessary. The pampered ladies of the fin de siècle were being overtaken by women with a more practical attitude to life and greater career aspirations. Women's lives were undergoing significant cultural change; in the new postwar world they were prepared to walk the streets without a chaperone, an action until then undertaken only by prostitutes. But as they shut the front door, leaving the security and comfort of the domestic world behind, women contrived to take some of its contents with them as a kind of psychological safety net. And bags themselves were changing to reflect the new world, a world of streamlined modernity, speed, and dynamism. They were to emerge sleeker and chic-er than ever before.

BELOW A more practical attitude to fashion begin to change the silhouette in the early twentieth century. As clothes became less decorative and shapes more streamlined, bags came more and more to the fore.

TWO

THE CULT OF THE CLUTCH

The more cultivated a people becomes,
the more decoration disappears.

LE CORBUSIER, C.1920[1]

BELOW LEFT *Art deco designers used cubist geometry to make accessories modern. A powder compact and tiny wrist bag of the 1920s are both streamlined and glamorous.*

RIGHT *The minimalist glamour of the 1920s encapsulated in an illustration from Vogue. The model wears a black crepe satin dress with a simple square clutch in black velvet with a jade clasp.*

In the 1920s, the fetid air of the stuffy Edwardian drawing room was left behind as women made their way into public life. The home was no longer their universe; heavy corsetry was shed and the appearance of voluptuous curves abandoned. This was the decade in which the bag came into its own, fashioned out of all manner of exotic materials and decorated with sequins, beads, and marabou feathers.

Streamlined clutch bags in Bakelite and Perspex looked to the future, encapsulating the modernist style. Clashing shades of emerald green and tango orange were inspired by the Ballets Russes, while the opening of Tutankhamun's tomb in 1922 led to a mania for Egyptian motifs. The drawstring bag was finally out of style; its pouch shape instead hung from a metal frame, heavily embellished for evening with Bohemian glass beads or fashioned out of plainer materials for daywear.

Modernism offered a new aesthetic for a new century, a new style arising like a phoenix from the ashes left by the Great War of 1914–18. Artists and architects, philosophers and poets alike believed that a culture that had allowed the carnage of the trenches to happen should be rejected outright and replaced, as design historian Penny Sparke expressed it, by "a different set of values from those which had underpinned Victorian society. In its cultural manifestations the desire to embrace the new was motivated by a burning need to reject the old and to move beyond Victorian culture, especially in its realist and historicist manifestations. For the modernists, Victorian culture stood at the end of history."[2]

Modernism prided itself on being outside of the historical moment, particularly in its rejection of the use of decorative devices that referred to past styles. Viennese architect Adolf Loos, whose writings profoundly influenced this new aesthetic, denounced unnecessary embellishment as a design crime, writing that "the path of culture is synonymous with the separation of the ornamental from the

LEFT *The fashionable woman of the 1920s portrayed by French fashion illustrator Georges Barbier as a cubist silhouette with the simplest of black clutches under her arm.*

BELOW *The drawstring bags of the early 1900s were completely rejected by the twenties flapper, who wanted the simplest shapes in which to keep her cosmetics. The flat sides of these typical clutch bags resemble mini cubist paintings.*

writer and fashion photographer Cecil Beaton. He recognized that an altogether more youthful type of woman with a slim silhouette and wardrobe to match was overtaking the fleshy courtesans of the Belle Epoque. For Beaton, Anita Loos, author of *Gentlemen Prefer Blondes* (1926), expressed this new look perfectly in her dramatic change of style:

> *In her early photographs, with the black shining hair dressed in heavy coils, she seems to be overwhelmed by the draped hats of velvet and sealskin, the voluminous coats, skirts, stoles and muffs of the first moving-picture era. But with the twenties, Anita Loos came into her own. The new fashions gave her the opportunity to become herself. She cut her hair as short as that of a boy in a sailor suit and went off to buy her hats and dresses at the juvenile departments of the great stores. Dressed as crisply and neatly as only a child at the outset of an expedition can be, her buckled belts and bag like a school satchel, her Buster Brown hats and Peter Pan collars, Anita Loos became the embodiment of cuteness.[5]*

Anita Loos's satchel-like bag embraced the functional aesthetic, the cornerstone of modernism, where clear simple shapes devoid of extraneous decoration were embraced and the frilly fussiness of Edwardian fashion rejected. Hermès, for instance, created a whole series of saddle-stitched bags with very simple shapes, such as the valise of 1923 and the car bag in 1925. But modernism needed to be allied with glamour in order to really take off. The minimalist *style du jour* began to be expressed most evocatively in the clean white angles of a Le Corbusier villa, the stark simplicity of a Bauhaus chair, and a little black dress by Coco Chanel. It was time for bags to fit more comfortably into this modernist mise-en-scène, to stop nestling against a softly upholstered hip. The look had to be cleaner, cooler, harder. And as a result, as fashion historian Farid Chenoune succinctly states, "the bag experienced the biggest change in its history."[6]

functional."[3] Woman's pleasure in ornamenting the self, he reasoned, would disappear as she fended for herself in the modern world and no longer relied on the rules of attraction to ensnare a man as provider. He continued, "We are approaching a new and greater time. No longer by an appeal to sensuality, but rather by economic independence earned through work will the woman bring about her equal status with the man ... Then velvet and silk, flowers and ribbons, feathers and paint will fail to have their effect. They will disappear."[4]

Loos's predictions were not entirely correct, but fashion did undergo a transformation, as identified by

Quite simply, the flounced, beribboned reticule was supplanted by the austere outlines of the *pochette* or clutch bag, a bag that snapped shut with a metallic "click." Its purity of design, simplicity of style, and streamlined geometry evoked a new era in which women were taking a more active role in society— and were prepared to declare it sartorially. The angular abstraction of a cubist painting was the perfect way to decorate the flat planes and angles of a clutch bag when designed by Sonia Delaunay or Jean Fouquet. The envelope flap of the clutch, in vogue from 1925 to 1930, became the soft suede or shagreen surface for jazz age sun-ray designs, the first monograms of fashion houses such as Patou, Lanvin, and Mainbocher, and even the most precious of Cartier gems. As Chenoune describes it: "Gripped by the upper arm or forearm, or carried in the hand in line with the body, [the clutch] was a traveling showcase

that flirted with the decorative arts and architecture. As a kind of portable painting imbued with the lessons of Constructivism and Cubism, the clutch bag represented a total break with the shapes of the past."[7]

Modernism could appear monastic in design terms, with its austere stripping-away of unnecessary detail. The Bauhaus philosophy of "form follows function" was just a starting point for some, however, and a faux functionalist aesthetic began to be applied to objects of material culture that weren't necessarily functional at all. The clutch bag is a case in point: A bag that appears to embody modernity with its clean lines and uncluttered appearance but is totally impractical for everyday use. Essentially a petite bag clutched under the elbow, it was too small to carry anything of any significance, easily dropped, and, by putting one arm out of action, physically restricting.

Clutch bags were also streamlined. This design trend was initially used for modes of transportation, but by the 1920s and 1930s, clean surfaces, rounded corners, and flowing lines were applied to all manner of objects to express the exhilarating fast new pace of modern life, and as a result, giving the impression of speed to objects that had no motion. Writer Dorothy Parker alluded to this in the mid-1920s, describing a chair that was,

> *… legless and short in back. It was a strain to see in that chair any virtue save the speeding one of modernity. Certainly it was a peril to all who dealt with it; they were far from their best within its arms, and they could never have wished to be remembered as they appeared while easing into its depths or struggling out again.*[8]

Bag design followed suit, becoming more aerodynamic and futuristic and being fashioned out of experimental materials with slick surfaces such as chrome, plastic, and Rhodophane, a derivative of glass that was brittle and transparent. The implicit sense of speed and progress inherent in this kind of industrial-looking material, together with the use of newly streamlined shapes, was also reflected in the

E DERNIER CRI DE LA MODE OU LE COMBLE DU RIDICULE

SACHA
ZALIOUK

fashions sported by the flapper—a *sportif* woman on the move with a cloche hat and clutch bag. Chic now depended on form rather than frill.

Loelia, Duchess of Westminster, remembered that "you couldn't help hearing flappers talked about. They were a novelty and they were news. Bishops denounced them. Old ladies deplored them."[9] Flappers were modern women of leisure who, according to popular imagination, were also libidinous and precocious. Cecil Beaton describes a new aggression in young upper-class women—or the "bright young things," as they were dubbed—and the popularity of the idea that it was smart to be rude, particularly to admirers:

> *If an unfavoured young man came up to talk to them, they would sit silently staring at their baffled victim and then suddenly burst into derisive laughter. They would leave the most grand and conventional dances early in the evening, to go on to night clubs. At house parties their highly powered motor cars were not infrequently driven through imposing gateways, breaking stone piers and filigree of wrought iron. One high-spirited young lady even managed to crack the bottom of an ornamental lake. Raucous, irritating and offensive as these young people were, they were undoubtedly the spearhead of those who broke down conventions.*[10]

Conventional appearance was a target and many sartorial rules were redundant. The *Daily Mail* recognized this in 1927, describing flappers as "slim as a lamp-post. The smiling dimple, for years a subject for poets and essayists and an inevitable accompaniment of the Victorian heroine, has disappeared from the face of the modern woman and is as rare now as the long skirt. Her face is harder. Her hair is bronze, her complexion vivid, her skin unwrinkled."[11]

The figure of Iris Storm, the tortured antiheroine of Michael Arlen's novel *The Green Hat* (1924), is one of the best-known examples of this radical twenties femininity. Storm is a sexually emancipated outcast, rejected by polite society yet

dazzlingly resplendent in green hat and yellow Hispano–Suiza car, which at the end of the novel she deliberately crashes, expiring dramatically in the ensuing conflagration. This is a woman out of male control, as disordered as life in the city itself. Storm's exotic sexuality is embodied in the fetishistic qualities of her bag, which is described by the narrator (soon to succumb to her allure) as "an oblong white-jade case, and chained to it by a double chain of gold was a hectagonal black onyx box which may or may not have held powder. One corner of the hectagonal black onyx was initialled in minute diamond letters; I.S. 'Iris,' she said. 'Iris Storm.'"[12]

A double bag fashioned out of exquisite materials and carrying both cigarettes and cosmetics was a daring concept in the early 1920s, suggesting that Storm, a woman with a wrecked reputation, cares little for contemporary etiquette and brazenly

flaunts two props that for many denoted the prostitute: A so-called painted lady who differentiated herself from a respectable domesticated woman by smoking cigarettes and wearing obvious makeup on the city streets. Storm is a woman who haunts Harlem drinking dens, dances the Charleston, and experiments with "free love"; a woman who travels light, who stalks the sidewalks alone in high heels and silk stockings.

Many women responded with enthusiasm to these changes: Virginia Woolf, for instance, writes of walking in London and reveling in "the swing, tramp and tread; in the bellow and uproar … in the triumph and the jingle and the strange high singing of some aeroplane overhead."[13] Women were finding freedom in the modern cityscape, including sexual freedom, and if such an urbanite as Iris Storm was no longer economically dependent on men, was this a new Amazonian race to be feared?

Freud, in his explorations of the human condition, attempted to understand this sexual uncertainty and the more complicated human relationships that had become a feature of modern urban life. He saw that femininity, for some, was a threatening spectacle: endlessly seductive, but at the same time a source of fetid neurosis that could leave men both psychically and physically diminished. In many of Freud's Viennese case histories, men were alienated from women, constantly running in fear of castration by urban viragoes.

In Katherine Mansfield's "The Escape," a short story written in 1920, Freud's notions of the psychic dislocation of modernity and the attendant anxieties associated with sexuality take material form in a bag. A husband is tortured by a demanding wife, who complains at every turn, seemingly too delicate to withstand the demands of daily life yet totally in control of their relationship. During one neurotic exchange he notices her bag lying on her lap, a "little maw … Its shiny, silvery jaws open … He could see her powder-puff, her rouge stick, a bundle of letters, a

LEFT *Modern femininity was, for some, seductive yet threatening. The clutch bag could appear as carnivorous as the flapper who carried it—in this case, Bette Davis.*

BELOW RIGHT *A silver cord evening bag plus long mesh gloves show a modern take on seduction typical of the 1930s—glamorous yet somehow deadly.*

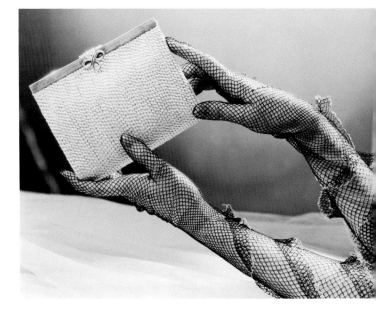

phial of tiny black pills like seeds, a broken cigarette, a mirror, white ivory tablets with lists on them that had been heavily scored through."[14]

The bag has snapping little jaws like his wife, constantly opening and closing, nipping here and there, a veritable *vagina dentate*. The castrating female with toothed genitals has always been a prevalent image in global mythology, symbolizing men's deep-seated fear of women. Here the bag becomes a symbolic castrator, an agent of the controlling woman who robs man of his masculinity by her constant wounding demands—and clues to her status are inside: the broken cigarette, the powder puff, and the rouge. The flapper's bag is carnivorous and man is destroyed.

The carnivorous clutch bag was made even more menacing by the application of a toothed zipper, "the alligator of ecstasy," as the writer Tom Robbins was later to refer to this modern mechanism of daily life.[15] First formulated in 1893 by the American inventor Whitcomb L. Judson as a device for fastening shoes, the zipper was soon fitted in gloves, corsets, tobacco pouches, and mailbags—or as Judson's Universal Fastener Company said, "wherever it is desired to detachably connect a pair of adjacent flexible parts": "A Pull and it's Done!"[16] It wasn't until the 1920s that the zipper was first applied to handbags, and in rather prosaic circumstances. As the historian Robert Friedel relates:

In 1923 the handbag framers of Manhattan, strongly organized in a union, went on strike, demanding considerably higher piecework rates (up to sixteen or even twenty dollars per day). The manufacturers resisted, and when it became evident that a slide fastener could be installed in a handbag by a seamstress without the benefit of a frame at all (in the manner of a soft-sided tobacco pouch), demand took off.[17]

Women were receptive to the zipper because of its modishness, so much so that Hermès began to make a feature of it in their luxury handbags. The zipper made evocative links with modernity, mechanization, and sexuality—a combination too powerful for the progressive woman to resist. Unzipping was becoming part of the erotic narrative, an action by which a lover could slowly reveal a woman's flesh at the side of the skirt, say, or the back of a dress. In 1932, writer Aldous Huxley in *Brave New World* described this gratification of uncomplicated desire in a future where zippers eased access to the body: "The zippers on Lenina's spare pair of viscose velveteen shorts were first a puzzle, then solved, then a delight. Zip, and then zip; zip, and then zip; he was enchanted. Her green slippers were the most beautiful things he had ever seen. He unfolded a pair of zippicamiknicks, blushed [and] put them hastily away again."[18]

The new zipped bag was used to carry cosmetics, and the practice of putting one's face on fueled its design. Lipstick, powder, and paint had once been a sure sign of disrepute, and in the early 1920s, many young women found it a struggle to buy the stuff, let alone leave the house with makeup on. In her novel *The Pursuit of Love*, Nancy Mitford revisits her youth and describes the trials and tribulations of trying to follow what was then a very daring vogue:

"We must get hold of some powder."

"And rouge."

These commodities were utterly forbidden by Uncle Matthew, who liked to see female complexions in a state of nature, and often pronounced that paint was for whores and not for his daughters.

"I once read in a book that you can use geranium juice for rouge."

"Geraniums aren't out at this time of year, silly."

"We can blue our eyelids out of Jassy's paint box."

We left our car in the Clarendon yard, and, as we were very early … we made for Elliston and Cavell's ladies-room, and gazed at ourselves, with a tiny feeling of uncertainty, in the looking-glasses there. Our cheeks had round scarlet patches, our lips were the same colour, but only at the edges, inside it had already worn off, and our eyelids were blue, all out of Jassy's paint box. Our noses were white, nanny having produced some powder with which, years ago, she used to dust Robin's bottom. In short we looked like a couple of Dutch dolls.

"We must keep our ends up," said Linda uncertainly.

"Oh, dear," I said, "the thing about me is, I always feel so much happier with my end down."[19]

As cosmetics began to be more widely marketed and readily available, so their use became a daily routine. Between 1909 and 1929, the number of cosmetics manufacturers in America doubled and women's magazines slowly moved from renunciation to capitulation on realizing they could generate a lot of revenue from advertising the varied products of Elizabeth Arden, Helena Rubenstein, and Max Factor. By the end of the decade, editorials were describing the changes that the use of foundation, rouge, mascara, and lipstick could bring, persuading women that the attainment of Hollywood glamour was not only possible but a certainty. In the *Ladies'*

Home Journal of 1927, for instance, Lynn Fontanne wrote that any signs of protest from a husband should be ignored: "In sending out this bulletin to American women, I want first of all to ask you to make up your faces. Study makeup. Put it on your faces frankly, boldly—but with artistry. Don't mind what your husbands say. Let them object as loudly as they please."[20]

As makeup became accepted, so did its application in public, even if many advice columns in women's magazines at first disapproved of public primping, seeing it as an example of "poor breeding." By 1934, though, the practice was so widespread that one French commentator remarked:

It has become difficult to differentiate at first sight an honest woman or a pure young girl from a whore … All women, from the adolescent to the grandmother, are moulded according to the same model; they wear lipstick and powder their faces, have pearly eyelids, long black lashes, painted nails, platinum or red hair …; they all smoke, drink cocktails, loiter at dancing halls, drive cars … how can we place them? Which is the marquise, the wife of the wealthy industrialist? Or simply the woman of easy virtue? What an embarrassing question and what a difficult problem to solve.[21]

As women's "face-fixing" drew attention to the fabrication of appearance—or as Kathy Peiss puts it, exposed "the artifice behind the illusion, the backstage of a woman's performance"[22]—bags became mini-pitstops in which repairs could be undertaken with an ostentatious unscrewing of a vial of perfume or the metal roll of a vermilion lipstick. Many began to take the form of miniature vanity cases, which needed to be more structured in order to hold the new products. At the same time, new materials entered the vocabulary of the bag, including celluloid, which could be molded into many different shapes. Reticules returned, this time in the form of mini lipstick containers that swung on lengths of chain or cord or were fixed to Bakelite

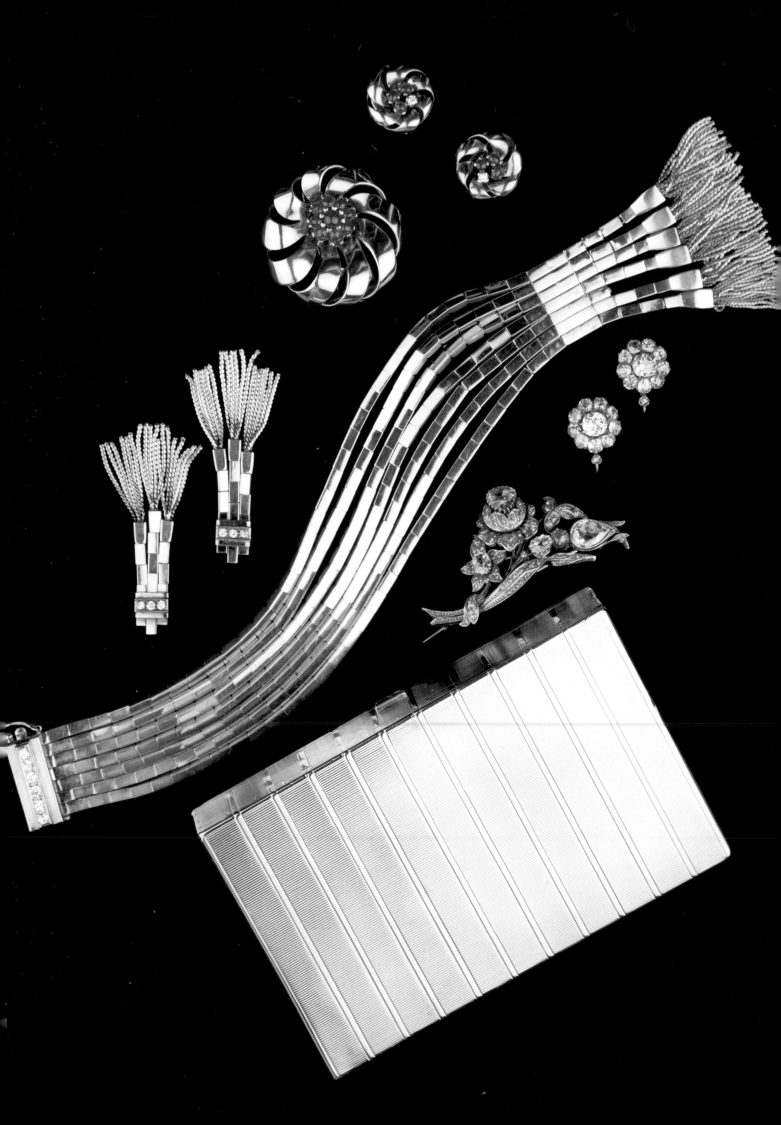

LEFT *Fashion photographer Cecil Beaton captures the thirties vogue for surrealism in his image of a model with a leather bag and suit with faux drawers by Elsa Schiaparelli, designed in collaboration with artist Salvador Dalí.*

BELOW *Schiaparelli introduced surrealist-inspired fantasy into her designs and kick-started the vogue for a bright shocking pink, after which she named her perfume.*

had made its first appearance in the poetry of Paul Eluard and Louis Aragon in the 1920s and the infamous paintings and performance art of Salvador Dalí. Surrealism celebrated the bizarre, the strange, and the hallucinogenic; Dalí's paintings caught on canvas the peculiarity of dream imagery, the product of the workings of the unconscious when allowed full play during hypnotic trance, drug-induced coma, or sleep. The unexpected juxtapositions of objects that poured forth from the imagination were dubbed "surrealist beauty" and are best expressed in the evocative description of the poet Comte de Lautréamont as "the chance encounter of a sewing machine and an umbrella on a dissecting table."

Paris was the epicenter of surrealist activity as well as fashion, so the two were bound to collide—as they did in the work of Italian couturière Elsa Schiaparelli. A feisty single parent from an intellectual Roman background, Schiaparelli designed clothes

and amazing accessories in a surrealist vein with chic-shock appeal for her legions of elegant clients. Fashionistas on their way to the Ritz Hotel would linger outside her boutique on the Place Vendôme, where bizarre window displays included a collaboration with Salvador Dalí in which a shocking-pink teddy bear with drawers in its torso balanced on a sofa inspired by Mae West's lips.

Schiaparelli designed hats shaped like high-heeled shoes, lamb chops, and exposed brains; buttons like clowns, and necklaces of aspirin—but her bags were witty examples of fashionable surrealism too. Throughout the 1930s, she variously produced, with the help of Dalí, Jean Cocteau, and designer Roger Model, bags shaped like a piano, a telephone, an apple of vivid red suede, a Chinese lantern, a lifebuoy, an umbrella, and a glass birdcage, all smoothly incorporating the surrealist notion of displacement into high fashion. A hat shaped like a shoe neatly turned the body upside down; a bag that looked like a folded newspaper transformed the throwaway into a treasured *objet de la couture.* Schiaparelli bags were surrealist sculptures, more for parading one's chic than carrying any humdrum objects—her transparent plastic abalone shell was one such example, as anything personal was in full public view. She acknowledged this with her "cash and carry" dinner jacket of the late 1930s, which provided its wearer with oversized pockets to carry everything her bags couldn't.

Emboldened by Schiaparelli's success, other bag designers started to abandon notions of modernist "good taste" in favor of witty creativity—parading difference was now more a la mode than being discreet. As Anna Johnson comments, "Suddenly everyone wanted a bag modeled after the shape of something utterly modern and zany. A leather clutch shaped like the *Queen Mary*, the Daimler automobile, the Lindbergh plane. Like a favorite soft toy, a figural pochette could be held close to the body, striking a witty contrast to a sober little suit."[25] Finnigans, an

important inter-war manufacturer, made a bag in the shape of an automobile with a door that ingeniously opened to reveal a mirror. Anne Marie of France created handbags in the form of a *trompe l'oeil* clock, a drum, a fan, and a Champagne bucket. Her roll-top bag in black felt opened using exactly the same action as an eighteenth-century roll-top desk, a perfect example of art historian Mary Ann Caws' definition of the surreal, where "nothing stays where it should or used to."[26]

A little functionalism entered Schiaparelli's bag design when, in 1938, she created the Lite-On or Lanterne handbag, again with Dalí. When the sleek expensive leather bag was opened, two internal light bulbs backlit a hinged mirror with a compartment for lipstick, alongside some fine Dalí engraving. This was not a new idea, as Dunhill's had attempted a Lytup

LEFT *Schiaparelli wittily inverted the functional aesthetic of the humble basket by making it a high-fashion accessory. This beachwear ensemble incorporating a woven straw bag dates from 1950.*

BELOW *Hollywood actress Karen Morley poses with a clutch bag with an internal light powered by its own battery for fixing makeup in dimly lit nightclubs.*

handbag in 1922, advertised in *Tatler* as "invaluable in a taxi or wherever the lights are dim,"[27] and Metro-Goldwyn-Mayer actress Karen Morley was photographed displaying a "Hollywood novelty purse" that contained a light powered by a battery that could be flashed on at night when she couldn't find her keys.

After all this experimentation, the beginning of the Second World War soon suppressed any design innovation in bags as practicality won out. Yet Schiaparelli refused to be ground down, believing that creativity could still flourish in adversity. Handbags could still be witty accomplices to their bearers, playing with class, social status, and fashion. This was not new territory for the designer. In the mid-1930s, Schiaparelli had perplexed the fashion cognoscenti by basing a print on newspaper, which she had seen twisted into simple hats by women to protect their hair while they worked in Copenhagen fish market. She then transformed this simple Danish

folk practice into luxury fashion, using the print on scarves, blouses, and bags.

Schiaparelli transformed the basket in the same way by removing it from the hands of the French laborer and transforming it into haute couture. However, although this fashion experimentation may have been "immediately all the rage" in occupied Paris, as Schiaparelli describes in her characteristically self-aggrandizing autobiography *Shocking Life*, the look didn't really cross European boundaries with any degree of success—as she discovered on a visit to the Prado in Madrid:

> *I had been told that the picture gallery had been completely rearranged in a fabulous way, and I wanted to spend an hour's relaxation with my life passions El Greco and Goya. As in Paris there was no more leather to be had for making women's handbags, I had taken some ordinary but pleasant-looking small baskets and lined them with cotton or chamois skins … I happened to be carrying one when I went to the Prado. The attendant stopped me and said: "No baskets are allowed inside."*
>
> *"But this is my hand-bag."*
>
> *A long discussion began. I refused stubbornly to leave my basket at the door because it contained all I possessed in papers and money. I asked for the curator and he came down immediately. He shook his head negatively. I then opened the basket and showed him what it contained. He still thought it was against the rules. I kept on repeating that this was all we could afford in the way of hand-bags and that anyway I could not hide an El Greco in it. Tired of arguing the curator allowed me in, but an attendant followed me the whole time, thus spoiling the communion with beauty that I was looking for and needed so much.[28]*

Schiaparelli's incomprehension of Spanish handbag etiquette had let her down, ruining her creative flow and confusing her peers. The rules were to be more clearly stated in the hidebound 1950s, when every self-respecting woman carried a bag—and by then the conventions were set in leather.

THREE
CARRYING COUTURE

*My mother's handbag was big and black
and aggressively pleated, with an
enchanting clasp in the form of two
parrots. The bag's richly dark interior held
the mingled fragrance of perfume and
leather – calfskin probably – and a cotton
handkerchief dabbed with "Evening in
Paris" wadded in one corner.*

CAROL SHIELDS[1]

Hostilities ceased, and a new era beckoned. What changes had been wrought by war? English writer Cecil Beaton surveyed the wreckage of the Blitz and was far from content. Women appeared tentative, their minds and bodies subtly transformed. And how did he know? They were carrying their handbags differently:

Thirty years ago pudgy little hands with dimples and pointed fingers were admired. Today the joints of the fingers are clearly discernible, and dactylar reactions are more nervous, highly strung like those little wooden hammers that appear if the corresponding piano key is struck. When a woman holds her handbag it is with her thumb sticking out at a tangent. Thirty years ago the thumb would not have been noticed, for it was discreetly hidden, with the purse held daintily by the tips of the fingers, the little finger crooked like a handle.[2]

Women were holding bags differently because accessories had changed during the 1940s for necessity's sake; pretty *pochettes* and glittering *minaudières* had no place in wartime Europe. Simplicity won out over surrealist excess, and the shoulder bag based on the military satchel became a common sight, swung across the torso of a female cyclist or worn with a black wool Utility suit. The American designer Claire McCardell even tried to persuade women to do away with bags altogether by concocting outfits with overlarge pockets in imitation of the comfort and ease of the male wardrobe.

American women did not partake in this kind of fashion experimentation because in their country conditions were a little different from those in Europe. Limited rationing had caused no real adjustment in women's fashion consumption. For most of the 1940s, the Adrian-designed suit accompanied by a large, structured, subtly expensive leather handbag from Hattie Carnegie's store in Manhattan was the glamorous uniform for life in the modern city. It was also the perfect look for shadowy film noir screen stars, for example Joan Crawford in

LEFT *Socialite Barbara Mortimer, known as "Babe Paley," displays the glamorous look that American women, free from wartime restrictions, adopted in the 1940s. Her elegant suit is accessorized with a flamboyant yellow bag.*

BELOW RIGHT *A black astrakhan bag from forties America—expensive, luxurious, and beyond the reach of many women.*

Mildred Pierce (1945). Writer Christina Stead described just such a woman in 1945, looking

> … *fresh and brilliant, her black hair piled in a braided crown. Her business dress, cut low in the bodice, was of silk shirred all over in two inch bands, tight in the waist and very short. She had steel studded buckles on her high-heeled shoes and long, black kid gloves. She threw her black astrakhan coat on the sofa, with an enormous handbag in calf and gold. She had a wide bracelet of brilliants, much perfume, and no colour in her cheeks but a dark red lipstick which brought out the darkness in her eyes.*[3]

It was this kind of large, luxurious, yet discreet handbag that was to dominate the 1950s. Women felt a patriotic duty to be well turned out after the war—bandbox smart with correct accessories to match—and the "good" handbag, as it was called, became a cultural obsession. A "good" handbag was modern, tasteful, and rationally designed, fashioned out of black calf, alligator, or crocodile skin. *Vogue* editor Edna Woolman Chase wrote in 1954: "Although a good leather handbag costs money, it is a sound investment. Antelope or suede are usually desirable."[4] And English beauty writer Betty Page wrote that same year: "Your handbag should have a plain uncluttered line that Americans adore."[5]

With the liberation of Paris in 1944, French haute couture reasserted itself. By the early 1950s, leading lights Christian Dior and Cristóbal Balenciaga were beginning to convince women that fashion had to be strictly followed. The fantasy many aspired to was Dior's New Look or Corolle line, which had originally hit the headlines in 1947 thanks to the sheer poetry and romance of its designs. With Dior, spectacular fashion re-emerged, richly embroidered and sensuously excessive with full crinoline skirts handcrafted out of yards of pale café-au-lait organza or champagne-colored tulle, all shimmering with mother-of-pearl embroidery. Elegant mannequins, throats lit by gleaming icy diamonds and sapphires, and hair sparkling with gold dust, presented an appealing vision to fashion-starved women who had been deprived of such finery during the war years. The model Jean Dawnay evocatively described a Dior show in 1950:

> *At 11 o'clock we started, and the babbling of the Press dropped to a breathless hush. As I passed through the grey satin curtains into the salon to show my first number, a caramel coloured fitted coat in grosgrain, I could feel the atmosphere of intense concentration like a tangible thing. There was very little room to turn and show properly, and when it came to the wider ball dresses with their yards and yards of tulle or heavy satin all sparkling with hand embroidery, one could hardly pass between the closely packed audience; the dresses dragged against their programmes and knocked ashtrays flying.*[6]

LEFT *The couturier Christian Dior in 1955, posing with examples of designs from his Paris atelier. In the foreground is a simple black evening bag.*

RIGHT *A chic Pierre Balmain ensemble from 1955 comprising a button-back skirt and black sealskin cape with matching handbag.*

Anne Scott-James, a fashion writer in the 1950s, wrote of how "a Dior opening would put journalists into the same state of frenzy as a fire or a bomb":

> *... the audience would be positively emotional, intoxicated with the beauty of movement and colour. Dior's mannequins walked in quite a different way from those at any other house. They neither minced nor strode athletically. They were taught to walk with a sort of pride, brushing the audience carelessly with their skirts as they passed, lifting their shoulders haughtily, walking rapidly, smiling at no one and stopping for no one. As the great skirts swirled, the pleats flew, the taffetas rustled, the embroideries sparkled and shone, the colours mingled and fused, even the hardest-bitten American would join in the French clapping and call "bravo" and "magnifique" and "ravissant."*[7]

Christian Dior had very specific rules about the correct handbag a woman should carry. He advised in his *Little Dictionary of Fashion* (1954) that "You can wear the same suit from morning to dinner – but to be really perfectly dressed you can not keep the same bag. For morning it must be very simple, and for the evening it must be smaller and, if you wish, a little more fancy."[8] Dior's insistence on "simplicity" for day belied the expense of what he was proposing: Day bags had to be luxurious, elegant, and beautifully crafted out of expensive skins such as python or ostrich. Like many other French couturiers, Dior did not design bags himself, but instead relied on the craftsmanship of established handbag manufacturers to complement his work; for him the dress was the focal point, all else was of secondary importance. At his atelier in Paris, after weeks of fittings, a rehearsal would be held, with the models dressed up in the new collection ready to be shown to the assembled press and public on the catwalk. It was at this meeting that the whole outfit would be completed with, as a Dior model described it, "Madame Bricard choosing the hats; Count Etienne de Beaumont selecting the jewels; Guillaume the coiffures and others the bags, furs, umbrellas and shoes."[9] This suggests that bags were low down on the pecking order at Dior, an important source of revenue that had yet to be recognized.

Slowly, a few astute Parisians began to realize that a couture handbag could provide an important finishing touch to a signature outfit—and could reach the women who couldn't fit into a couture jacket or afford an extravagant evening gown. An affordable alligator clutch adorned with a *griffe*, or designer label, allowed far more consumers to buy into the fantasies associated with a particular label and, most importantly, to assure them that what they were buying was "good." As Ginette Spanier, director of the house of Balmain, explained: "Women need the sense of security that the *griffe* gives them."[10]

Women were, of course, content to buy bags with a *griffe* inside to avoid the sort of faux pas that had almost ended Spanier's own career at Pierre Balmain, one of the most prestigious Paris houses of the 1950s. Although fully understanding the rules of fifties haute couture, Spanier seriously slipped up in one of her early meetings with the couturier:

BELOW LEFT *Despite the age gap, two generations of the British royal family carry almost identical white leather bags in 1959. From the left: Queen Elizabeth, The Queen Mother, and far right, Princess Margaret.*

In the hysteria of the Couture all standards are topsy-turvy. If a seam is not quite right, that is a matter of life or death. If a woman is not soignée enough (that abused word means "well-groomed", but mere "well-groomed" falls far short of the standards of the Couture, let me tell you) it is a tragedy of melodramatic intensity. I remember appearing once with Pierre Balmain when I thought I really looked marvellous. Hair, shoes, dress were all perfection. Pierre Balmain screamed. "Ah-h-h," he screeched, "your bag. It's terrible." [11]

Unfortunately, in her autobiography she gives no details of the grotesquerie that had provoked such a heated reaction.

Thus it was in this period that many iconic couture bags, complete with the magical *griffe*, appeared, including Chanel's legendary 2.55, named after its month and year of birth. Coco Chanel's idea for a practical shoulder bag was originally mooted in 1929, when "sick and tired of holding my handbags and losing them, I stuck a strap on them and wore them slung across my shoulder." [12] Her first shoulder bags were made of black or navy jersey and, when revisited by the designer in 1955, became objects of luxury and desire with the introduction of quilted leather, gilt fastenings, and the ubiquitous long gilt chain handle interlaced with black hide. Inside, the bag was still eminently practical with three discreet flap pockets: one for lipstick, one zippered for security, and one totally secret, perhaps for the adoring *aides-mémoires* of a lover.

The Hermès Kelly bag was another icon of handbag design that rose to prominence in the mid-1950s. Handcrafted out of two alligators, the belly of the beast for the body of the bag and the more flexible neck skin for the sides, the Kelly bag was originally introduced in 1935 as a "small tall bag with straps." Celebrated owners included screen legends Marlene Dietrich and Ingrid Bergman. But it was not until 1956 that the bag's reputation became positively stratospheric. Film star Grace Kelly had given up her

successful career in Hollywood when she married Prince Rainier of Monaco in 1956, a union some said was predicated on economic necessity rather than love, as Rainier had decided that the publicity attached to marrying a famous blonde would attract tourists to his tiny cash-strapped principality. His first choice of bride, Marilyn Monroe, turned him down but Grace was prepared to agree—despite the fact that Rainier insisted on her family paying him a $2 million dowry. Kelly's virginal Waspy image was a facade astutely promoted by her studio to hide very effectively an earthy sensual woman, who had been courted and squired about Hollywood by some of its most eligible bachelors (and a few of its married men), including Clark Gable, William Holden, Bing Crosby, Ray Milland, Gary Cooper, and David Niven. She became pregnant by Rainier in the same year as the wedding and was famously photographed for the cover of American *Time* magazine shielding her swelling belly with a classic Hermès bag—thereafter known as the Kelly and still a best seller today.

The Hermès Kelly, considered the Rolls-Royce of handbags, is still instantly recognizable and incredibly covetable. The 2004 film *Le Divorce* played on its expensive allure: In this romantic tale set in Paris, Kate Hudson begins an illicit affair with a much older married French aristocrat, who seals the deal with an Hermès Kelly in red, a gift he offers every lover at the start of an affair. This is significant, because only sixty Hermès Kelly bags are created each season and the waiting list is long, at least three years; clearly this man either has some standing to obtain a bag so easily, or, with some degree of cynicism, has planned his liaisons way in advance.

Hermès justifies the expense of its Kelly bag—$4,000 for the most basic model—by explaining that each bag is handmade from start to finish and includes more than 2,600 hand stitches, a signature flap closure with an engraved gold buckle, and four tiny gold feet on which the bag stands in order to prevent the three layers of skin that make up the bottom from wearing out. Its understated look is said by some to exude "old money." Vintage handbag dealer Inga Guen goes one step further: "A woman who is going to wear the Kelly is of very erect stature, she comes from money, a very good background, is extraordinarily educated, and life to her is one where she will be very inconspicuous."[13]

The idea that a woman carrying a Kelly bag was bound to be inconspicuously elegant was certainly less spurious in the 1950s. In this decade a chic couture bag was a sign of "good breeding," especially when coordinated with the "costume" or two-piece suit. The fashion tip of the 1950s, endlessly repeated by fashion editors in incessant advice columns, was to invest as much money as one could in a bag, as it would then last a long time and detract attention away from clothes that were perhaps a little less exclusive. As beauty writer Joyce McKinnell put it in *Blueprints for Beauty*: "Concentrate on an immaculate appearance and better accessories. Good handbags, shoes and gloves are worth pounds to you in looks, even if you cannot afford an expensive suit,"[14] and Dora Shackell advised in *Accent on Accessories* (1957): "A good handbag is something one can afford to be snobbish about; it is so very much a sign of good grooming. A real telltale, open or shut."[15] To be "frankly feminine," as one beauty writer put it, all one needed was artistic flair in order to collect "really good accessories almost like jewels. If you can afford a special present, lizard or snakeskin is hard-wearing, good-looking and almost as luxury looking as crocodile, though one third of the price."[16]

LEFT *A red leather handbag by Pauline Trigère designed in 1952. Trigère was a French-born American couturière whose glamorous Hollywood-inspired fashion styles made her one of the most successful designers of the 1950s.*

BELOW *Fifties women were besieged by advice from beauty editors on how to achieve the correct look. Here, women are given tips on how to walk with a handbag.*

Vulgarity was to be avoided at all costs, McKinnell explained in a chapter entitled "Deadly Faults":

> … *[it] often happens when a woman tries to act or talk on a level with the opposite sex, telling doubtful jokes and, in general, completely disregarding the fact that she is a woman. Remember that it is also vulgar to talk loudly in public places, such as cafés or on buses, or to sit with your legs crossed and showing your new blue suspenders.*[17]

Intimations of vulgarity could strike when one least expected it; the "tall woman," for instance, "should beware of handbags which are over-large and clumsy, rather than plain handsome … large handbags often make her unnecessarily conspicuous and unfeminine."[18] Constance Moore in *The Way to Beauty* (1955) had advice for the chubby, informing that the "lavish effect" of a large bag is "fatal to the plump woman."[19] Small women could encounter problems too, according to Eileen McCarthy: "A small woman with tiny hands and feet and a small head will look swamped by a large handbag … Good taste and good fashion depends to a great extent on a sense of proportion in all things."[20]

Ginette Spanier gave a good illustration of just how a vulgar bag could give away a "bad" girl in public:

> … *crocodile was suddenly the fashion. All the tarts had to have crocodile straps, shoes, handbags (the bigger the better) because crocodile was much more expensive than any other leather. One girl won the crocodile match hands down. She asked for a crocodile wardrobe trunk and she got it. It was enormous, it weighed at least a ton, it had gilded corners and looked astonishingly like the Albert Memorial.*[21]

And it wasn't just the bags themselves that could make one's lack of fashion know-how blatantly obvious to others; the way they were held in a woman's hands was equally telling:

> *Consider your friends and how you would improve their appearance and their wardrobes, but I would advise you to use the utmost discretion in your findings! Can you remember how six of your friends carry their handbags? (By the way, how do you carry your own? Remember?) Do they clutch them for fear of a sneak-thief – squash under the arm to the detriment of both bag and coat – sling from the shoulder to bang into the faces of other luckier travellers who have got their seats in a crowded bus – dangle from two fingers? Handbag carrying is an art because a bag should be a final touch to an outfit.*[22]

LEFT *A Lucite bag, hand engraved with birds and flowers, complete with a rococo-revival handle: A bizarre mix of the eighteenth century, chinoiserie, and modern technology.*

RIGHT *A color-coordinated outfit from 1956 shows the importance of matching accessories in this decade. One had to be smartly groomed at all times with matching hat, shoes, and handbag.*

However, all this invaluable advice could prove to no avail if one couldn't crack the code or—perish the thought—had a sudden momentary lapse, perhaps while relaxing on vacation. Travel writer Emily Kimbrough describes a case in point when detailing her friend Margie's handbag faux pas in Milan in 1955:

We went to the opera … on our way through the foyer to the bar for a glass of champagne, walking slowly, and we hoped elegantly, something swinging at Margie's side caught the eye simultaneously of the other three.

Sophy voiced our mutual wonder. "What in the name of God is that?"

Margie hauled up the object in her hand, not in itself an easy thing to do. It was the largest knapsack handbag I think I have ever seen, and it was of bright mustard-coloured leather. With this, Margie was wearing a dress of black lace and chiffon in clinging lines, large and very beautiful diamond pendant earrings, matched with a dazzling breastplate. We queried Margie about her choice of evening bag.

Margie's eyes are as blue and candid as a child's. She looked from one to the other of us. "Why," she said, "I didn't think anyone would notice it." She strode ahead of us toward the bar, swinging vigorously by the handle the mustard beauty.

We huddled close together as we sipped our champagne … we suddenly felt we had been dressed by the village dressmaker.[23]

There was a lot for fashionable ladies to take on board. The choice of handbag was obviously fraught with danger and one needed wise counsel to get it right. Accordingly, the purchase of one's first "good" handbag became a rite of passage marking a girl's metamorphosis into a woman and a moment when mother's advice was always best. Writer Carol Shields remembers it as a defining experience:

I was twenty when my mother took me to buy my first shoulder bag. This was the mid-1950s, when shoulder bags had been off the fashion list for years, but I was going to Europe to study, my junior year abroad, and my mother seemed convinced that a quality bag was essential for the security of my belongings. We found the perfect bag in a downtown department store. The price was $11. My mother handed over her charge plate, and turned to me murmuring, as she always did when shopping, "Now, don't tell Daddy how much it cost."

But on the day we brought the lovely new shoulder bag home we neglected, for some reason, to remove the price tag. "Well," he said at last, "this is a very good bag. And a very good price too."[24]

Up until the mid-1950s, fashion remained relatively conservative, with teenage girls dressing in a similar style to their mothers in little veiled hats, kid gloves, and suits or shirtwaist dresses—essentially watered-down copies of French couture or American ready-to-wear. Young women looked to the rather middle-aged, groomed elegance of *Vogue* models such as Carmen del'Orifice and Dorian Leigh for inspiration and copied their heavy makeup, overstyled hair, and matching accessories. At some point, there had to be a change—and it was the teenager who broke free. Economic booms in both Europe and America meant that teenagers had more money and more leisure time in which to spend it and, most importantly of all, more freedom to experiment in their social lives. This was recognized in a 1956 article entitled "Have Girls too much Freedom?" In his polemic, St. John Irvine described how the rules of conduct were changing and voiced several words of caution:

Today, some parents, though not by any means all, allow their daughters to go unaccompanied and unquestioned where they please, returning late at night, without any sort of escort, even though their journey home may take them through dark and dangerous streets. In my boyhood, no woman was allowed to walk away from a party without an escort. Today girls go almost anywhere they like.[25]

Young women were going out to the new espresso bars and Soho nightclubs, listening to modern music, and becoming ever more anxious to differentiate themselves from the fashions of their mothers and all the stiff and starchy etiquette associated with the formal fifties look. A new generation of young adults—now dubbed teenagers—were beginning to create their own coffee-bar culture. As Penny Sparke explains: "Young people rejected the 'middle-aged' values of their elders and demonstrated that it was possible to combine technocratic, progressive culture with 'fun' and style-consciousness."[26]

The bag, in particular, was associated with an older generation, with its qualities of function and longevity rather than feminine frivolity. British fashion expert Marnie Fogg remembers this well:

My mother's bag seemed to have a real history even though it would have been relatively new in the mid-1950s. It was all worn at the edges and had a soft, furry suede inside that smelled of Coty powder and Yardley perfume. She carried mints and a little flask for brandy with a silver top in case she felt faint or travel sick but never keys because the door was always left open. Her bag was sacrosanct because that's where her purse was and it was off limits. I wouldn't have dreamed of going in her bag – it would be like going in her underwear drawer.[27]

One of the lifestyles that teenage girls looked to for inspiration was that of Hollywood film stars such as Doris Day or Jayne Mansfield. The latter lived in pastel pleasure in Bel Air in an ersatz Mediterranean villa filled with all the latest modern conveniences. Pink was the color that identified this particular brand of conspicuous consumption. It was used in interiors (Jayne Mansfield's house was so steeped in the color that it was dubbed the Pink Palace), car design, even kitchen essentials such as the refrigerator and oven. A color so associated with femininity was, of course, perfect for that most feminine of objects, the bag. The manufacturers of plastic bags, in particular, used pink to create futuristic fantasies in toughened plastic—the embodiment of postwar optimism.

In 1931, chemical researchers at DuPont had created a new tough plastic derived from petroleum that they trademarked Lucite. Its first uses were military—nose cones and windshields for bombers during the Second World War and gun turrets for fighter planes. After the war, Lucite was injection molded or more expensively handcarved and used for decorative items such as jewelry. But its most famous incarnation was handbags in a range of cute colors, such as avocado, champagne beige, or blue pearl, in ornate, rococo-revival designs with carved handles, etched bodies, and filigree keyholes.

Plastics had been used in handbags before, but usually in imitation of other materials, particularly leather, alligator, and crocodile. Semiologist Roland Barthes suspected that this use of plastic "indicated pretension," and that plastic objects "belonged to the world of appearances, not of actual use; aimed at reproducing cheaply the rarest substances, diamonds, silks, feather and furs, silver, all the luxurious brilliance in the world." Barthes went on to analyze how, in the 1950s, plastic was beginning to "climb down by becoming a household material … for the first time artifice aims at something common not rare."[28] But Lucite was never that prosaic when used in handbags. Indeed, it was used in the construction of some of the most bizarrely eccentric yet astonishingly beautiful handbags of the twentieth century. The Lucite handbag represented new

FAR LEFT *The generation gap is made clear at this London bus stop. The chignon has been replaced by a shorter "easy" hairstyle and the "good" bag rejected by this teenager in favor of a gimmick.*

LEFT *A 1958 take on surrealism. A young woman wears bejeweled hands as hat and handbag while wearing gloves. Teenagers regarded their mother's handbags as rather staid, preferring the cheap and cheerful.*

technology, a resplendent object in the sophisticated jet age where it seemed anything was possible. This was the bag as bizarre hybrid, able to marry space-age materials (anticipating the sixties mania for all things plastic) with the high femininity of the boudoir to create an uncompromisingly modern yet still highly crafted version of the reticule.

Pastel pinks and blues, oyster, and pearl gray were the most popular shades in Lucite handbag design, usually studded with faux jewels or inset with plastic flowers, sea horses, glitter, or confetti as manufactured by Llewellyn, Wilardy Originals (famed for their "quick-release" closure), Dorset Rex, Charles S. Kahn, Patricia of Miami, and Rialto. Shapes veered from rectangular through bucket to pagoda and beehive, some bags so big they functioned as mobile dressing tables with scalloped edges able to accommodate hairbrushes, rollers, and makeup kits and incorporating a mirror in the hinged lid.

The most intriguing Lucite bags were totally transparent, the idea being that the owner could wrap up all her belongings in a colorful scarf, which could be changed to coordinate with each outfit. This was breaking every rule of twentieth-century handbag design. Bags were supposedly secret spaces —this was a purse as peep show. Brash, almost brassy,

more akin to British sex symbol Diana Dors than Doris Day, this bag was as shameless as its owner, or so it seemed in fifties pulp fiction. In *Living It Up*, a naughty novel of 1955 set in the Haven holiday camp during "the wild weeks of the summer," Hannah Sole, a "misunderstood lovely who thought she could tell what any man wanted," makes her entrance:

> *The front door creaked open. All eyes turned toward it, like compass needles toward magnetic north. And there she was: tall, white-blonde, honey skinned. She stood lushly framed in the doorway pretending she'd never seen the place before. Then she floated across the big room on a wave of perfume that threatened to displace the entrenched stink of Bowery stiffs … She pranced by, highly glossed, sleek, making impudent little scrapes with her spiked-heel shoes. She was caressed by a tight-fitting, white knitted suit. The arched elastics of her panties screamed out against the white skirt. And all male vitality was seduced out of the atmosphere like gas siphoned from a huge tank. Her transparent handbag oscillated cutely under her wrist, the colorful bits of claptrap jangling inside like a kid's kaleidoscope under a full head of motion. Our eyes met. I was gone.*[29]

Hannah's revealing bag complements the seductive exposure of her underwear, making visible that which was normally kept hidden. This kind of bag was unquestionably sexy; as writer Mary Elizabeth Williams put it, "Who wanted alligator pocketbooks anymore? Hell, gators have been with us since the dawn of humanity."[30]

The experimental use of Lucite came at a cost, however, both economically and practically. Such bags were pricey—sold in high-end department stores, they could cost up to a week's wages in some cases—and the experimental nature of the material meant that there were a few problems that couldn't be resolved. The bags had to be kept out of the sun because any degree of heat caused them to warp and, in some instances, leak liquid Lucite, which, of course, had implications for the owner's health. One collector wrote: "Avoid Heat! The odour-emitting Lucite bag you have lying around the house could KILL YOU! … The gas stings eyes, could cause allergic skin reactions … bloodshot eyes, bad complexions and terminal maladies."[31]

Lucite bags could also crack and shatter, but this was not the only reason for their fall from grace in the 1960s. Collector Sara Cameron recalls:

The top designers of the day (notably Will Hardy and Charles S. Kahn) were constantly trying to out-do each other by implementing more and more extreme features onto each handbag: rhinestone detailing was at a premium for the glamorous, and Wilardy embarked on a series of glow-in-the-dark bags that allowed women to see into their purses in the darkness of the theater. The result? Lucite bags were getting more and more bizarre, and consequently, more and more expensive to make.[32]

The rise of the teenager, and the recognition by manufacturers that young women wanted products to express a different persona to that of their mothers, meant that handbags were now being targeted at two quite different markets. Teenage daughters in the 1950s wanted a bag that represented the verve of rock and roll, the spirit of the jive, and the freedom of a new postwar generation. The first of many fantasy fifties bags, the Wilardy Confetti Lucite vanity case, in oyster or champagne beige, fitted the bill perfectly; its futuristic Perspex lines were the female equivalent of the brash dynamics of a Chevrolet's tailfin.

As the decade wore on, more and more bags specifically targeted at teenagers were being produced, not necessarily high-quality or long-lasting, but cheap, brash, and fun. Breaking all the rules of fashion etiquette, these bags could be used by girls during the day as well as at night. French poodles were a popular motif, not only on bags but also on plates, curtain material, and skirts; when emblazoned on a bag they could make the owner feel like a fantasy film starlet fresh from the beaches of St. Tropez. The poodle was soon joined by a host of other animal motifs, including elephants, frogs, and fish, occasionally fashioned out of wicker or hand beading and usually made in Japan.

By the end of the 1950s, there were plenty of bags to choose from: leopard skin for the femme fatale; leather for the elegant woman about town; red velvet for evening; ostrich for day. Silk cord, Belgian beadwork, carved and etched Lucite, sleek patent leather—what did this rampant handbag mania say about women? Lawrence Langner hazarded a guess in 1959 in his celebrated tome *The Importance of Wearing Clothes* (1959). Langner had a goal: to explain the psychological imperative behind dress and how this affected fashionable trends in the modern world. Handbags were particularly interesting, he felt, because their increased number, size, and weight seemed to reflect the increased visibility of women in the public arena in the later years of the decade. He wrote of:

… the emergence of the handbag, an article of utility and luxury carried by women not only to show their superiority over other women, but also their ability at weightlifting. The modern woman of fashion disdains the idea of pockets or pouches to carry anything in her clothes. And for good reason. She is already hard put to cover at least four portions of her body which tend to protrude through her clothes and proclaim the femininity from which she is often hopelessly attempting to escape. Shall she add a fifth to this in the form of a purse or wallet, which can be carried by hand? And to this the handbag owes its popularity which is growing greater each year as woman increases her importance as a social being … As she becomes increasingly engaged in women's clubs or business activities, the bag grows bigger, since it now must contain copies of speeches, pamphlets, MSS, a mailing list and a filing system. Pockets indeed! The lady will soon need a private wheelbarrow![33]

LEFT *Bags became as brash as the decade itself, sculptural shapes in pastel colors that symbolized modernity in the same way as a gull-winged Chevy.*

BELOW *The clutch bag continued as an elegant staple of every fashionable woman's wardrobe in the 1950s but moved from day wear to evening.*

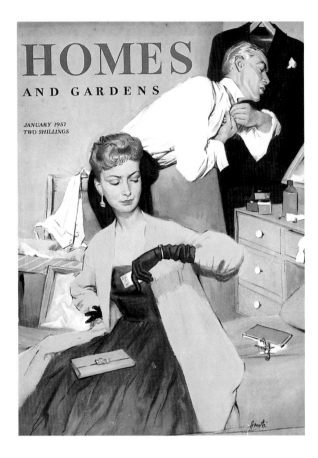

Langner anticipated sweeping changes in women's lives and, consequently, in their relationships with their bags. He foresaw a rejection of traditional femininity and an ever-increasing involvement by women in the practicalities of life, as opposed to the "trivialities" of fashion. Feminists Simone de Beauvoir in Paris and Betty Friedan in the U.S. were also documenting this process, predicting a wholesale rejection of the fashion system as women began to understand the political nature of their oppression. The 1960s were to bring great changes to women's lives; this would indirectly affect their handbags and their attitudes toward them, which would veer from abject love to downright rejection. At any rate, they would no longer be prepared to accept the handbag in its predominantly conservative fifties form.

FOUR
FAST-FORWARD TO THE FUTURE

The fifties had been so sinful, so old.
In my twenty-first birthday photograph
my dark lips, vaselined lids, tightly waved
hair, stiff black dress and pearl necklace
age me poignantly; but by the time I reach
thirty I'm dressed like a Kate Greenaway
child in white stockings, flat shoes and
high waisted dresses, with my cropped hair
I look about twelve years old.

ELIZABETH WILSON[1]

LEFT TOP *Mary Quant's "first crack at handbags," as she described them, are simple yet stunning exercises in op art.*

LEFT BOTTOM *Spanish models dressed in op-art-inspired clothes accessorize with swinging shoulder bags in 1966.*

RIGHT *A model shows off the new range of Mary Quant shoulder bags with matching travel bag at a 1966 trade fair.*

In 1959, a seismic shift in pop culture was felt in the offices of British *Vogue*. "Young," they announced, was now "the persuasive adjective for all fashions, hairstyles and ways of life."[2] Chelsea girls, crazy dollies, cool modernists, and stoned hippies were at the epicenter of an out-and-out "youthquake,"[3] when to be young was to be in command. Or at least it seemed that way when writer John Corsby announced in 1964 that "suddenly the young own the town."[4]

Teenagers had become the new arbiters of style, challenging and transforming mainstream fashion and, consequently, bag design throughout the decade. As Marnie Fogg writes in *Boutique*, her seminal book on sixties fashion, "Fashion ceased to be a peripheral activity and became central to the experience of being young, attractive and cool."[5] The notion of individuality flourished. This newly emergent generation were "absolute beginners," as writer Colin MacInnes dubbed them; girls and boys who, draped in their casually elegant "teenage drag," realized that "for the first time since centuries of kingdom come, they'd money, which hitherto had always been denied to us at the best time of life to use it, namely when you're young and strong."[6]

Fashion, and concomitantly fashion accessories, became an important focus of this liberal self-expression as the established order of things was questioned and disavowed. The stranglehold that French haute couture had held over female taste seemed, for many, to be released upon the death of Christian Dior in 1957, and Italian style emerged as its successor, with magical names such as Gucci, Pucci, and Ferragamo signifying youthful cool and modernity. In London, the designs of Mary Quant were pivotal, sparking a sartorial revolution and marking a definite change in style for women as one decade merged into another.

Quant, often described as the fashion equivalent of the Beatles, had opened Bazaar, one of the original boutiques in London's King's Road, in 1955. As she

LEFT *Twiggy was a massive influence on teenage fashion in the 1960s. Here she holds a large mock-alligator box bag.*

RIGHT *A shoot for* Vogue *in 1966 shows the op art influence on high fashion complete with Vidal Sassoon-inspired geometric haircuts.*

explained, "I had always wanted the young to have a fashion of their own … Absolutely twentieth century fashion."[7] She later reflected: "To me adult appearance was very unattractive, alarming and terrifying, stilted, confining and ugly. It was something I knew I didn't want to grow into."[8] Quant's clothes were totally different from the refined chic of the French couturiers. Her inspiration derived from sports, school uniforms, and childrenswear, which in her hands evolved into candy-striped rugby shirts, woolen knickerbockers, and pleated pinafores worn with knee socks.

The presentation of a Quant catwalk show was as deliberately provocative as the clothes. Models no longer haughtily paraded; that was for the French fashion elite. Quant's designs had a different vibe, as was made clear when they were shown for one of the first times alongside the established grandees of the British fashion world, Victor Stiebel, Mattli, and John Cavanagh at the Palace Hotel, St. Moritz. As Quant remembers:

The whole atmosphere was electrified. There was a stunned silence. Everyone stopped eating and drinking and talking. The thing was that they were expecting to see nothing but the grand clothes of haute couture … The music changed to hot jazz. The girls pranced down the stairs, one after the other, wearing little high-waisted flannel dresses with white stockings, or alternatively, flannel tunics over red sweaters with red stockings to match … Grown-ups wearing teenage fashions and looking like precocious little girls.[9]

This girlish, childlike quality was extended to Quant's initial handbag designs. Two rare prototypes are illustrated in her 1965 autobiography *Quant by Quant*, captioned: "My first crack at handbags." These designs are of the utmost simplicity: abstract circles of black and white derived from the monochromatic op art experiments of painters Bridget Riley and Victor Vaserely—paintings that were to be plundered by many designers throughout

the decade and used on products as diverse as dress fabric, sunglasses, and album covers. Quant's promotion of an exaggeratedly childlike aesthetic reinforced the idea that fashion was for the young, an endorsement made clear in another early handbag design using her trademark daisy motif, which resembled the first doodlings of infancy.

According to Quant, designs such as these symbolized the breakdown in the barriers of age and class that had so dominated the 1950s:

There was a time when clothes were a sure sign of a woman's social position and income group. Not now. Snobbery has gone out of fashion, and in our shops you will find duchesses jostling with typists to buy the same dresses … The voices, rules and culture of this generation are as different from those of the past as tea and wine. And the clothes they choose evoke their lives … daring and gay, never dull.[10]

But top model Twiggy had a different perspective, observing that Bazaar was always "for rich girls."[11]

LEFT *In contrast with the youthful bag designs that dominated the 1960s, this high-fashion model poses with an elegant leather bag for those with more sophisticated tastes.*

RIGHT *British pop singer Lulu in a multi-colored geometric print hat and matching chain-linked shoulder bag from 1967.*

Twiggy's assessment may not have been entirely objective, as, first, she was a working-class girl from the suburbs of London, far removed from the Chelsea cocktail-party set who were the early patrons of Bazaar, and second, she was a mod. Mods were among the most sartorially ambitious of the new teenagers: Fashion fetishists absorbed with the details of their clothes, which were worn as a form of modernist body armor in a rather stuffy postwar Europe. Mod boys wore sharply tailored Italian mohair suits, reflecting a very visual culture in which elegant good taste was no longer the preserve of an educated elite but was moving from the ground upward—from sidewalk to catwalk rather than the other way round. Mod girls were just as pristine, sharp, and elegant. In her memoir *Baggage*, journalist and television producer Janet Street-Porter remembers the meticulous detail that life as a London mod demanded in 1964:

> *I was seventeen, and looking suitably fashionable was all-important, and so I spent hours slaving over a sewing machine to get exactly the long narrow look that suited me. My skirts were long and narrow and covered my knees with kick pleats at the back, and I teamed them with square-toed shoes with high thick heels from Raoul, a shoe shop in Soho. I would make tailored over-blouses to go under my leather jacket. I made shift dresses that were cut in at the shoulder, skimmed the hips, had piped collars and pocket details. Handbags had to have long straps, your hair had to be sleek and chopped. It was a very precise look.[12]*

In this extract, Street-Porter cites the shoulder bag as the bag of choice for the mod girl, worn "swinging" (like the eponymous 1960s themselves) from the shoulder against a backdrop of hissing Gaggia espresso machines or the cool Blue Note tunes of a Soho jazz club. Mod girls posed with bags that had been rejected by their mothers in the 1950s as a symbol of wartime austerity; for a sixties teenager, shoulder bags kept the hands free for living and loving. Shoulder bags became a symbol of liberation—at its most evocative in the opening scenes of the film *Billy Liar* (1963), when Julie Christie is introduced as Liz, a free spirit visiting a stolid northern town, who wanders its sooty streets with her hair uncombed, defiantly swinging her bag, having made her escape from London.

As skirts got shorter, bag straps got longer, almost in compensation, and the shoulder bag or satchel (another forties staple) became an integral part of the little-girl look when worn insouciantly across the chest. Marnie Fogg remembers that "the early to mid sixties silhouette was really pre-pubescent and bags which little girls used were popular—dolly bags, satchels … and always slung like a child diagonally over the torso to leave the hands free. The bags we chose were never remotely elegant, chic, or ladylike, not ever constructed."[13] Worn with a geometric Five Point haircut by Vidal Sassoon and adopting the "droopy, helpless, rather gormless pose that was then all the rage,"[14] as model Valerie Thurlow put it, the look was original and brand spanking new.

Not everyone followed the look so prescriptively. Twiggy was one of the few teenagers to carry her

shoulder bag a little differently from the in crowd around this time. She recalls being asked out on a date by a local boy, Christopher, who arranged to meet her at Wimbledon railway station and then on to a night at the cinema:

> *I went along so excited, in a black and grey double-breasted coat with an imitation leather collar, all the rage then, and a small black shoulder bag that I carried under my arm … Well, I got there, and I waited and waited and waited. Twenty minutes, half an hour went by, me standing holding my bag under my arm, and three trains came in, and then nothing, and then I went home … the phone rang and it was him … He'd got there twenty minutes after I'd left, because something had happened on the line and they'd all had to get off the train and be transferred into coaches. The stupid man at the station hadn't told me there were no more trains coming in. Christopher had asked him whether he'd seen me. And the funny thing was, Christopher said to me, "Did you have a dog with you?" Because the guy at the station had seen me clutching this black thing – my bag – under my arm![15]*

Recognizing that there was money to be made from the new teenage revolution, established department stores began to open their own teen departments—a kind of boutique within the environs of the parent shop—in which accessories played a major role. Buyers had to rethink their policy on bags, however, as expensive versions had a dated image and resulted in many young girls rejecting them out of hand. One teenager of the early 1960s remembers: "I never bought a handbag in the sixties. All I carried was a lipstick and ten Kent cigarettes. I occasionally used a forties envelope bag in soft brown leather or carried shoppers I made myself out of a length of furnishing fabric. I didn't aspire to a handbag, I associated that with my mother or royalty and wearing gloves."[16]

Even fashion editors recognized that the handbag might become defunct. Claire Wilcox observes: "between 1961 and 1966 handbags hardly featured in fashion spreads, for they simply didn't look right … At risk of losing their entire business, handbag manufacturers were forced to respond to ever changing vogues, and the quantity of mass-produced, ready-to-wear and disposable fashion set a new tone."[17] Patent leather had the glossy looks that could tempt the young woman. Sylvia Plath wrote of buying a pair of "size-seven patent-leather shoes in Bloomingdale's one lunch hour with a black patent-leather belt and black patent-leather pocketbook to match."[18] But, as patent leather was out of the reach of most teenage purses, plastic became the trend-setting material of the decade.

PVC, or poly-vinyl-chloride, was one of the first plastics to be used in sixties fashion. It became particularly popular after the space-age experiments of a group of designers based in Paris—Emmanuelle Khanh, Paco Rabanne, Pierre Cardin, André Courrèges, and Rudi Gernreich. These so-called *ye-ye* designers (from the French pronunciation of the Beatles's "yeah, yeah, yeah") were responsible for rebranding the French look, badly needed by the

LEFT *The 1960s was an optimistic decade in which fashion designers experimented with an array of new materials. This model poses in a metal chain-link dress by Joan Arkin.*

BELOW RIGHT *French fashion designer Paco Rabanne's iconic chain-mail bag was a revolutionary re-run of the Edwardian mesh reticule.*

1960s as many houses were stuck in the fifties mode, tightly organized under the auspices of the Chambre Syndicale de la Couture Parisienne and showing their collections in secret so that their extravagant designs couldn't be copied by the hoi polloi.

Residual products associated with designer names, such as sunglasses, perfumes, and bags, were seen as the way forward, real money-spinners that could save struggling fashion houses from closure. Such goods were also more suited to what many believed was a more egalitarian decade. Since the early 1950s, Dior and Balmain had been branding products with their monikers, then selling them to stores under license. Balmain model Valerie Thurlow remembered Dior accessories marked for the English market that were "mostly manufactured in Bethnal Green, London, emblazoned with the magical name of the master, and subsequently sold for a small fortune … who can blame a house for 'going commercial' in this commercial age?"[19]

For a more widespread shake-up of French couture, though, a complete turnaround in the public's perception was needed. Fashion had to be fresh, it had to presage the future—and that future had to be now! Cardin was first out of the block in 1964 with his Space Age collection, which featured white knitted catsuits, tabards worn over leggings, and tubular shift dresses. Emanuel Ungaro wasn't far behind in 1965, when, as journalist Richard Morais describes, "He went on a silver binge: silver wigs; silver-soled boots; silver buttons, collars and mesh stockings … Aluminium necklaces doubling up as bras were juxtaposed with see-through flower-appliquéd trousers."[20] Courrèges showed space-age chicks in laboratory-white conditions in helmets, huge white goggles, and flat-heeled white glacé boots modeling clothes in a restricted color palette of white, red, and black. Meanwhile, Pierre Cardin's Cosmonaut collection, appearing at the height of the space race, dominated the headlines, described as "a sort of ski outfit for the cartoon family, the Jetsons. A

blouse was tucked into nylon-like ski pants that were again tucked into heavy black boots. The look was topped off with a Newfoundlander's cap. When, in 1969, Neil Armstrong walked on the moon, Cardin gasped, 'You see, I was right.'"[21]

This science-fiction trend changed the appearance of bags—white patent leather, plastic, and PVC creations appeared in the shops and in most other areas of cultural production, such as the set and costume design of the popular British television series *Space 1999*, Verner Panton's injection-molded plastic chairs, London's Post Office Tower, and Joe Colombo's lighting. Paco Rabanne claimed that there were no new frontiers left in fashion save the discovery and use of new materials. He totally broke with tradition by experimenting with plastic and aluminum to create chain-mail bags, a sixties version of the Edwardian mesh reticule. It was estimated that by 1966 Rabanne was using 100,000 feet of Rhodoid plastic per month in his bags and jewelry, which included such

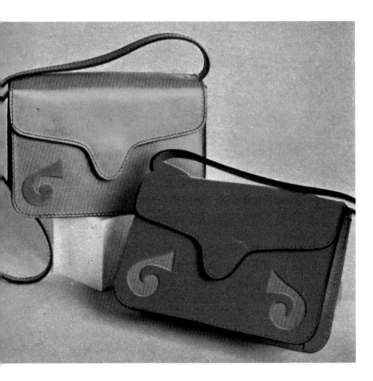

extraordinary artifacts as a bib necklace made of phosphorescent plastic discs strung together with fine wire. When he had exhausted the possibilities of plastic, Rabanne created another version of chain mail using tiny triangles of aluminum and leather held together with flexible wire rings to construct a series of simple shift minidresses and purses.

It was a look that went global. Andy Warhol described its New York invasion, in particular when sported by his Factory superstars, including the infamous Edie Sedgwick: "The kids in the Dom looked really great, glittering and reflecting in vinyl, suede, and feathers, in skirts and boots and bright-colored mesh tights, and patent leather shoes, and silver and gold hip-riding miniskirts, and the Paco Rabanne thin plastic look with the linked plastic disks in the dresses."[22] Warhol recalled that 1967

> … *was the year of the electric dress—vinyl with a hip-belt battery pack—and there were lopsided hemlines everywhere, silver quilted mini-dresses, "micro-miniskirts" with knee socks … crocheted skirts over tights—to give just the idea of a skirt. There were big hats and high boots and short furs, psychedelic prints, 3D appliqués, lots of colored textured tights and bright colored patent shoes.*[23]

By the mid- to late-1960s, bags could be flat with cutout handles, portable Union Jacks that embodied the spirit of Swinging London, tiny "go-go" bags that swung from the wrist when dancing, "wet look" when coated with polyurethane, and the antithesis of the fifties "good" bag, crafted out of toughened paper with its own built-in obsolescence —just like Max Clendenning's disposable cardboard furniture. Bags were upbeat, off the wall, and gimmicky; all they needed was to have immediate impact. The mentality was, as one fashion journalist observed, "enjoy-it-today-sling-it-tomorrow."[24] The comic strip, gaudy colors of pop art could be found in even the most grown-up of bags: Those from Gucci could be ordered in a stunning lemon yellow

BELOW *Among an older generation, the expensive designer bag never went out of fashion and was to re-emerge in opposition to the hippie- inspired ethnic styles that dominated youth culture.*

FAR RIGHT *A selection of Coach bags designed by Bonnie Cashin in the 1960s. From top, a red crushed cow hide A-line tote, a red leather See-Thru tote, and a green Cashin-Carry.*

or white patent leather, while Pucci bags were available in gold-and-tangerine leather with a velvet or silk body vividly patterned in a rainbow of psychedelic hues, including lime, ultramarine, and turquoise.

Bonnie Cashin's bags for Coach turned the company—established in 1941 and famed for its good-quality leather pocketbooks—into one of the leaders in bag design and manufacture in sixties America. In Cashin's words, her bags were "punchy": a riot of bright primary colors—rich lipstick reds and grassy greens with striped Madras cotton interiors— but still functional and hard-wearing. The witty Cashin-Carry models, for instance, had built-in purses that were situated either inside or outside the bag for ease of access; the bag then closed with a brass toggle. Her leather totes were large and flat: she experimented with packability, trying to refine the bag down to its most practical essentials, and several bags of different colors were meant to be layered one over the other on the arm when shopping in New York. As Cashin put it, "My strong personal feeling is to banish the word 'match'"[25]—that belonged to the previous generation.

Culture could accommodate excesses such as these. The ethos of Carnaby Street in London or the Upper East Side in New York was, like that of any other agglomeration of shops, capitalism incarnate— the drive was still to spend, spend, spend, even if the customer demographic had changed. As new markets opened up and affluence continued to be paraded through rabid lifestyle consumption, male fashion

LEFT *A shopper browses in a boutique in 1971, sporting a wet-look bag complete with poodle .*

RIGHT *Two models pose in Dior outfits fashioned out of plush bohemian velvet with Dior logo-ed luggage in 1969. The designer label was to dominate the next two decades of bag design.*

with women presenting their bodies as delicious packages to be unwrapped. Women were supposed to seduce through their dress, not men. But in this new age of egalitarian utopianism, fashion began to cross gender boundaries—hair, for instance, became androgynous as both men and women grew it long and wore it unstyled and natural, "floating around their heads like smoke," as feminist Germaine Greer evocatively described it.[27] Some designers went so far as to maintain that a truly unisex fashion was possible in a decade that seemed so culturally and scientifically advanced—and this new look for men had the potential to be beneficial for all mankind, not just a styling device for an episode of *Star Trek* or some fantasy space-station on Mars.

In *The Rag Dolls*, "an electrifying novel about today's world of fashion" written in 1968, which "digs behind the scenes of the kinky boutiques of Chelsea … where the narcissism of the boys almost outdoes that of the girls," gay couple Corry and Julian show off their latest outfits: "Everyone was examining the clothes they were wearing: they were both in transparent plastic jumpsuits, with small white bikinis underneath. A group of people near them applauded. Others whistled. 'Ladies and Gentlemen!' Alex shouted dramatically, 'I'd like to present *Ragtime's* new look for men: the see-through look.'"[28] It is significant that in this extract the models of such avant-garde fashion are gay, as if only "effeminate" men could perform sartorial statements such as these.

In the cold light of day, few men were prepared to blur the boundaries between male and female dress. Liberal attitudes to fashion were all very well in private, but it was a different story when the two most suggestive of fashion items from the female wardrobe —the skirt and the bag—were proposed as suitable attire for the modern man in the swinging city. Jacques Esterel was one of the first designers tentatively to put a toe into these dangerous sartorial waters. Born in 1918, Esterel was a true fashion pioneer and showman, perhaps best known for

became a new hothouse of invention out of which pranced the "peacock male." This was a man far more obviously interested in his looks than most and no longer content with being the foil to his exquisitely dressed wife. Andy Warhol described men who had become jaded with "straining to compete in glamour and marketing with women's fashions." He felt that "this signalled big social changes that went beyond fashion into the question of sex roles. Now a lot of men with fashion awareness, who'd been frustrated for the last couple of years telling their girlfriends what to wear, could start dressing themselves up instead."[26]

Masculinity, or at least masculine clothing, was being redefined in an era of more liberal sexual expression, the acknowledgment of a gay identity, and the rise of radical feminism. The cultural construction of gender, particularly when it was expressed sartorially, was being questioned—and about time too. It was the moment for men to become the decorative sex.

In the past, dress and accessories had been seen as women's offensive weapons in the battle of the sexes,

designing actress Brigitte Bardot's "Vichy" bridal gown. In 1964, he decided that the models for his catwalk show would have shaved heads "to give new importance to a woman's face."[29] Two years later, he designed a "skirt suit" for men in Dacron check. Rudi Gernreich followed not far behind, with citrus-yellow miniskirts for both men and women. He predicted that by 2000, "Clothing would not be identified as either male or female. So women will wear pants and men will wear skirts interchangeably."[30] As skirts had few, if any, pockets, a logical extension of this interest in cross-gendered fashion was to get men toting bags.

The subject of handbags, of course, had regularly surfaced in arguments regarding gender and dress—the suffragettes' rebuttal of reticules and demand for bigger pockets in women's clothes is a case in point. In the 1960s, the opposite occurred: A few like-minded men began to insist on bags, albeit a very small group of avant-garde men in Paris. The Group of Five, founded in 1956 by tailors André Bardot, José Camps, Max Evzeline, Socrate, and Gaston Waltener, was set up with the goal of creating the equivalent of haute couture for men. From the late 1950s until 1968, the five showed twice-yearly catwalk collections at the Crillon Hotel, Paris, in which they presented lavishly embroidered waistcoats and parrot-colored dinner jackets with vibrant, almost luminous linings in modern materials such as Tergal and Dralon. One of the group's most notorious ideas was the proposal of a closer-cut suit that hugged the body and, according to Farid Chenoune,

> *… obliged them to eliminate all pockets that might detract from overall elegance, notably the left inner pocket—or wallet pocket—of the jacket. At least one of the two hip pockets on trousers was also dropped. This move would have gone practically unnoticed if they had not made a corresponding suggestion, far bolder at the time, that men therefore carry a handbag or "man-case" as the press dubbed it in an unfortunate choice of words that condemned the initiative to nothing other than brief notoriety.[31]*

The term *man-case* alluded to the briefcase rather than the handbag to give it a more appropriately masculine-sounding edge, but, like the male skirt, it was not a resounding success. It was the nonconformity of the hippie movement and the general acceptance of the peacock male into the mainstream that made man-bags acceptable a little later in the decade. By then, the extreme tightness of men's bell-bottom trousers made the man-bag inevitable, as men needed somewhere safe to keep their small change without crushing their testicles.

slogans in ink on a bag, all denoted an individual approach to style: Now the brand you were advertising was yourself. Designer labels represented commodity fetishism at its ugliest and should be avoided by any self-respecting Marx-spouting radical. Unsurprisingly, the classic French bag came under attack, this time by the anticapitalists of counterculture. In Jean-Luc Godard's *Weekend* (1967), the Marxist film director mused on the decadence (and probable collapse) of the bourgeoisie while telling the tale of cynical couple Roland and Corinne. Having decided to murder her father for his inheritance, they set off across France in his classy Facel-Vega sports car and immediately become embroiled in a gargantuan traffic jam. The car, in Godard's hands, becomes the ultimate symbol of capitalist decadence as the couple pick their way through an apocalyptic landscape of smashed vehicles and broken and bleeding bodies. Corinne's alienation from daily life is finally revealed when their sports car is destroyed in a head-on collision. As Roland pulls himself, wounded, from the blazing wreckage, she screams out in anguish, "Help! My Hermès handbag!" This is her only show of real emotion throughout the narrative.

In Godard's hands, the bag becomes a defining image of countercultural demonstration—something unimaginable at the beginning of the decade—and a presage of the 1968 student riots in Paris. It was not to end here, however. Beatle John Lennon and artist Yoko Ono had something to add. In 1968, they hit upon the idea of using the bag as a metaphor to debate racial prejudice and sexual stereotyping in a crusade they gave the collective name Bagism. John Lennon announced that by completely covering oneself with a bag—literally inhabiting it—you became invisible. Nobody could prejudge you by your appearance; no one could tell the color of your skin, your age, social class, or financial status—all barriers of communication could be broken down and any words spoken would be pure and direct.

Lennon and Yoko Ono's first appearance as Bagists occurred on stage at the Albert Hall in 1968. Enveloped in a large black velvet bag, they remained inert for 45 minutes. (Although the tiny movements occasionally detected were gleefully interpreted by the press as evidence of sexual activity, the couple denied any amatory exploration when questioned afterward by journalists.) A Bagist performance was also staged for a press conference in Vienna in 1969, when the couple sat in a white bag eating chocolate cake. Bagism's aims were explained in a television interview with David Frost on July 14, 1969. Lennon attempted, at length, to clarify his new movement to his jocular host and a mystified studio audience:

Lennon: "What's Bagism? It's like ... a tag for what we all do, we're all in a bag ... I was in this pop bag going round and round in my little clique, and she was in her little avant garde clique going round and round, and you're in your little tele clique and they're in their − ya know? − and we all sort of come out and look at each other every now and then, but we don't communicate. And we all intellectualize about how there is no barrier between art, music, poetry ... but we're still all − I'm a rock and roller, he's a poet ... so we just came up with the word so you would ask us what bagism is, and we'd say WE'RE ALL IN A BAG BABY!

Frost: You've got a bag there with you, what do you do with it?

Lennon: Well sometimes we get in it, and sometimes other people get in it ... if people did interviews for jobs in a bag they wouldn't get turned away because they were black or green or [had] long hair, you know, it's total communication ...

Frost: ... They'd get turned away because they were in a bag ... [36]

Was Lennon right—could bags truly change the world for the better? Could peace and love prevail? The next two decades were to prove otherwise. Capitalism triumphed, avarice was au courant, and the bag became a decadent object of luxury and desire.

FIVE

LOGO-MANIA

Everything is power and money
and how to use them both …
We mustn't be afraid of snobbism
and luxury.

DIANA VREELAND (1980)[1]

LEFT *Feminist Germaine Greer saw the*
handbag as a symbol of women's servitude.
In Lord Snowdon's portrait of 1971 she
poses in front of two typically sturdy
examples of seventies bag design.

BELOW *A radical feminist demonstration of the early 1970s symbolically crucifies tokens of women's oppression including an apron, stockings, and a mesh shopping bag.*

RIGHT *The Enny bag was the first choice for the fashionable feminist. Lovingly crafted out of supple leather, it was built to last.*

Nineteen-seventy was a year of disenchantment. The optimism of the so-called Swinging Sixties was nowhere to be found as the Beatles broke up, rock stars Jimi Hendrix and Janis Joplin self-destructed, and the war in Vietnam continued despite voluble protest across the world. Taboos were still there to be overcome, including sexual ones, despite the liberalism promoted by the Love generation. Richard Neville, editor of the underground magazine *Oz*, admitted that

> ... *the marginal increase in society's promiscuity content, detected by various pollsters, is not about to shatter the foundations of Christianity. In a brief investigation, I discovered that an unmarried couple could still not (without lying) book a double room at Claridge's, obtain a chalet at a Butlin's holiday camp, migrate to Canada or book a double berth on a P and O liner.*[2]

A resolute and vociferous protest had been brewing, though, and in that same year, Germaine Greer's dazzling feminist tract *The Female Eunuch* was published. In her polemic against patriarchy and capitalism, Greer targeted the fashion system as one of many cultural institutions that dominated and suppressed women, particularly in its insistence on promoting beauty ideals that were impossible for ordinary women to live up to. Modish clothes that revealed the body's curves transformed women into trivialized sex objects, she claimed, and because women were concentrating on primping and preening themselves, they were left with no time to fully understand the nature of their oppression.

The fashion system was also guilty of carnage, Greer continued, by artificially creating a demand for beautiful objects fashioned out of precious materials plundered from nature. She visualized rampaging men on reckless quests to seek out the raw materials for handbags, among other unnecessary objects of decadent luxury, pillaging and destroying everything in their wake. The resulting accessories were then

used to bedeck the "Eternal Feminine," an injurious archetype of whom Greer wrote:

The sun shines only to burnish her skin and gild her hair; the wind blows only to whip up the colour in her cheeks; the sea strives to bathe her; flowers die gladly so that her skin may luxuriate in their essence. She is the crown of creation, the masterpiece. The depths of the sea are ransacked for pearl and coral to deck her; the bowels of the earth are laid open that she might wear gold, sapphires, diamonds and rubies. Baby seals are battered with staves, unborn lambs ripped from their mother's wombs, millions of moles, muskrats, squirrels, minks, ermines, foxes, beavers, chinchillas, ocelots, lynxes and other small and lovely creatures die untimely deaths that she may have furs. Egrets, ostriches and peacocks, butterflies and beetles yield to her plumage. Men risk their lives hunting leopards for her coats, and crocodiles for her handbags …[3]

Feminists, including Greer, Evelyn Reed, and American Dana Densmore, were particularly incensed at fashion's preoccupation with youth, and their arguments made perfect sense when juxtaposed with the ugly posturing of certain Parisian designers around this time. In an interview with *Penthouse* magazine, for instance, Pierre Cardin castigated rich older women (a little remiss of him, given that they were some of couture's few customers), declaring that:

Ageing women with their stupid desire to please make the work of pioneering creative designers extremely difficult … Whenever we produce something a little daring or unusual, public opinion starts to scream. "This is ugly! This is obscene!" Of course it is if seen on the body of some old hag … In the nineteenth century Balzac gave women thirty years as the limit of their emotional and sexual life. Let us not be over-generous today and double this figure in order to feed the female vanity … I'm not concerned with youth pills, rejuvenation clinics, face-lifts, and silicone injections. If there is one thing I hate it is vulgarity – and there is nothing more vulgar than a middle-aged woman disguised as a hippy or, as we say in French, a "ye-ye" girl![4]

It is no wonder that women began to question what fashion had to offer once they were out of their twenties. Their rebellion expressed itself in rejection of cosmetics, the bra, the bag—anything that was recognizably feminine. Hands were kept free as bodies were clothed in functional workwear with substantial pockets, in particular painter's canvas trousers and dungarees, and the much-vaunted argument of bags versus pockets began again in earnest, to continue throughout the 1980s. American feminist Susan Brownmiller, for instance, wrote: "Rarely does a woman experience the liberty of taking a walk with empty hands and arms swinging free at her sides. So rare is this, in fact, that many women find it physically unnerving when they do. Unaccustomed to the freedom, they are beset by

BELOW *Robert Capucci has been one of Italy's leading fashion designers since the 1950s. These alligator and crocodile bags from the 1970s have his unmistakable stamp of Roman luxury.*

BELOW RIGHT *Barbara Bolan revived the clutch bag in the 1970s and 1980s. Her trademark scallop-shell design took inspiration from thirties Hollywood.*

worries that some needed belonging (a purse, a shopping bag?) has been forgotten."[5]

As if in penance for their sixties space-age flippancy, bags in the early 1970s were determinedly serious: an array of earnest satchel shapes adorned with long-abandoned craft practices such as poker work. Fashion was taking refuge in nostalgia as the continuing war in Vietnam, the political scandal of Watergate, and worries about the ecosystem created a sense of disillusionment that hung about the early years of the decade like a specter at the feast. An understated, rather tweedy English style—all hacking jackets, Fair Isle sweaters, and riding boots—appeared on city streets, which seemed less metropolitan and more and more the new center of pastoral pursuits. Mulberry was an important purveyor of this bucolic look. The company was established in 1971 to sell the accessories of Roger Saul, including a range of bags that took their design motifs from traditional rural sports such as hunting, shooting, and fishing—

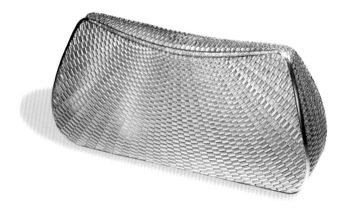

not the most egalitarian of subjects, but still popular because of their references to traditional craftsmanship and utility. Saul described the designs as "romantic but robust."[6]

Feminism was gradually becoming incorporated into mainstream culture. Ironically, its radical slogans and enlightened objectives of independence and equality for women were co-opted by the advertising industry as a way of selling products such as Charlie perfume. The cigarette brand Virginia Slims, for instance, told women, "You've come a long way baby," branding itself as an appropriately feminist smoke, while Enny, an Italian manufacturer of leather handbags, marketed itself as a purveyor of "Bags for Today's Women." Feminist Abigail Healey remembers totally renouncing bags in 1970, but the Enny bag caused her to pause and reconsider her radical stance:

I had stopped wearing make-up in the late sixties and early seventies as I didn't want to be regarded as a sex object or victim of fashion. I needed a way of carrying more stuff in the mid seventies though and liked the satchel shapes that were around—they seemed practical rather than fashionable. The first really nice handbag I had was an Enny and it came from Italy. It was well designed, had buckles and straps, was a good size and lined in suede. You couldn't get bags like this in England so I kept getting it mended. I kept it until it literally fell apart.[7]

The bag had become a utilitarian tool; it would have to break out—monotony, and not a little worthiness, were setting in. At first, fashionable bags looked backward, taking refuge in retro as fashion veered through a series of romantic looks inspired by prewar styles. The most successful of these was, of course, Biba, whose department store opened in London in 1973. Edwardian reticules and thirties-inspired clutches by Clive Shilton were a powerful antidote to hippie fringed affairs or sober styles in sturdy leather for the serious-minded feminist.

It would take disco to really sex up the bag, however, and by the light of a glitterball, the dissolute, decadent 1970s were born. Disco went mainstream in 1975, after, as music journalist Mark Jacobson wrote:

… black and gay people, two embattled cultures, adopted the forlorn dance halls and transformed them into the most dynamic form of entertainment since Hendrix set his guitar on fire … The clotheshorses were out; the new scene was all kinky eight-inch platforms, luminous make-up, and outrageous sexuality. It soon became clear that these discos, which were quickly renamed "par-r-rties", were for, as The Jackson 5 say, "Dancing, dancing, dancing machines." And madness ensued.[8]

Infamous New York clubs had names deliberately dripping in exoticism—Liquid Smoke, the Cobra, the Jungle. The most spectacular of all, wreathed in clouds of Yves Saint Laurent's Opium, was Studio 54, which launched in 1977 and closed two years later. Occupying a disused television studio on West Fifty-fourth Street, the club instantly became the place to be seen for the celebrities of the day, including Liza Minnelli, Andy Warhol, and Cher, who was pictured on the front page of the *New York Times* on opening night gyrating on the 11,000 square-foot dance floor while Bianca Jagger made an appearance on the back of a white horse in a cloud of glitter dust. Less infamous sequinned divas kept their money (and cocaine) safe in feathered plastic necklace purses by Fiorucci or brandished metal mesh clutch bags by Whiting and Davis. The high-octane glamour of metal discs shimmering under the strobe lights of the latest hot club made mesh appeal to a new generation, both male and female, who started to wear matching mesh tops, ties, and bandanas.

The zeitgeist was excess, the mood carnivalesque, as all manner of polymorphous perversities were played out by glistening bodies clad in spandex, Lurex, body glitter, and lip gloss. This Dionysian anything goes attitude was reflected in a penchant for fashion with an element of fetishism—leopard skin, killer heels, and black leather—and was perhaps best expressed in the

look of the doomed bisexual supermodel and heroin addict Gia Carangi, a favorite with photographers Guy Bourdin and Chris von Wangenheim, whose work encapsulates the excesses of the disco era.

The handbag that best articulates the raw sexual subtext of Studio 54 was by Carlos Falchi. A true genius of handbag design, Falchi originally hailed from Brazil and started life as a designer in the film and music industry, creating flamboyant stage costumes in patchwork leather for Mick Jagger, Cher, and Tina Turner in the late 1960s. At night he worked at Max's Kansas City, a restaurant-cum-bar-cum-club that had been the foremost salon of the psychedelic era in the late 1960s and a haunt for superstars and speed freaks by the early 1970s. It was here that Iggy Pop rubbed shoulders with David Bowie and the Velvet Underground and the New York Dolls played their first live gigs. The chic outrageousness that characterized the venue became a distinctive quality of Falchi's bag designs too with their decadent and luxurious mixes of pink crocodile, shiny black python, and lipstick-red lizard skin.

In 1974, Falchi produced a truly inspired handbag, the Buffalo, a cross between a handbag and a duffel bag. This bag was seriously sexy, an organic folded shape whose deep creases of leather seemed to mimic the hidden folds of the female body. As Falchi explained, "... bags were very stiff in the '60s, more like weapons than accessories. I would take my leathers and dye them in the bathtub at home using crazy Aniline colors. Nothing matched and they were very light[weight]. At a time when everybody was crying out for freedom, I made bags that swung, that moved and caressed the body."[9] It was a bag that invited a suggestive glance and a sly touch, a bag built for frottage or the stroke of a whip, a bag fit for peroxide-blonde punk princess Debbie Harry or to be photographed as still-life by enfant terrible Robert Mapplethorpe. This was the bag that presaged punk rock, the aesthetic of anarchy and subversion that was to dominate the late 1970s.

Falchi's bags were survivors; as he expressed it: "I want to be able to squash and trash a bag and still see it keep going." [10] His creations could last a lifetime of debauchery, many surviving intact after 30 years. Yet their punk qualities belie the fact that these bags are luxury items, handcrafted out of a sensuous blend of luxury skins in unexpected and vivid color combinations. In the early 1980s, Falchi produced a series of dramatic leather clutch bags with multi-colored lizard inserts, mixing purple, violet, and olive green or shards of copper and silver metallic snakeskin. Butterfly bags of deep caramel reptile skin with buttery brown leather or soft black suede linings were an experiment with the bag as a "vessel"—a primeval shape used for carrying the essentials of life rather than the fripperies of consumerism and fastened with a drawstring, which created deep, earthy folds.

Falchi's sculptural investigations were the exception in the late 1970s, however, as the bland branded bag began to prevail. Fashion writer Georgina Howell was remarkably prescient in 1975 when she wrote: "In the 1960s clothes hinged on age. In the 1970s they will hinge on price." [11] Quite ordinary bags, for instance, could be marketed with higher ticket prices if the signature of a well-known designer was displayed in the form of a logo, and Pierre Cardin, in particular, began to brand practically everything in sight. By the 2000s, long after his heyday, well over 800 products still bore his name. His ambition was to be a living label: "My name is more important than myself." [12] As Henri Berghauer, one of Cardin's top managers, commented, "He wanted to be Renault." [13]

Throughout the 1970s, Cardin licensed his name to suit and shirt manufacturers, womenswear, and accessories, including ties, scarves, jewelry, and bags, which were manufactured in Italy and at first sold in his new boutique in Milan. Objects peripheral to fashion and more to do with lifestyle followed: Pozzi ceramics, office toys, furniture, even collapsible bikes.

By 1974, *Time* magazine was describing Cardin as "the most successful practitioner of design proliferation … a shrewd fantasist who has tacked his name onto just about anything that can be nailed, glued, baked, bolted, braced, bottled, opened, shut, pushed, and pulled." [14] Never one to miss a photo opportunity, Cardin posed for the cover wearing nothing but a pair of Cardin socks, his modesty saved by … a discreetly placed Cardin towel.

Pierre Cardin truly democratized the designer brand, but at the same time he provided a salutary lesson for those only too happy to follow his example. In the 1960s and early 1970s, the name Cardin conjured up an image of cutting-edge, forward-looking chic. By the late 1970s, however, after a series of worldwide licensing deals, the Cardin brand had started to become devalued. Although the licenses may have been personally lucrative for the designer, the result was that more and more merchandise bearing his name began to appear on the market over which he had no direct control. Too many inferior products were on sale in duty-free shops, and that magical sense of exclusivity began to disappear. Apocryphal stories abounded, such as that of the bottles of Cardin wine selling for $2.99 each, which were allegedly so noxiously acidic that the corks disintegrated on contact, or the rather undignified series of "futuristic" free-form handbags in the shape of a woman's buttocks, which, quite unsurprisingly, proved a little difficult to sell. Cardin may have become a multimillionaire, but it was a Pyrrhic victory. Historian Daniel Boorstein explains:

If designer labels are really successful, and reach larger and larger markets, they become so democratized that everybody wears them. And then they become franchised for hamburgers and everything else. People want to benefit from the prestige of the Cardin label, but of course prestige quality has been destroyed. The destruction comes not because no one wants the Cardin name, but because everybody wants the Cardin name. [15]

Counterfeiting was also rife; not many manufacturers could resist the quick buck to be made from faking a logo. The problem was exacerbated by considerable advances in technology in the 1970s that enabled many of the original craft skills used in the production of handbags to be superseded by industrialized processes. In addition, many businesses were moving their manufacturing bases to poorer countries to take advantage of the low cost of labor—and those prioritizing low labor costs did not tend to be particularly interested in intellectual property rights. All this meant that convincing copies of deluxe designer bags manufactured in Thailand and sold by street vendors from Hong Kong to Berlin began to flood the market. Gucci, among others, paid the price, with a brand that became increasingly tarnished.

Other designers took over as the must-have labels of the fashionable elite, some of them relaunches of classic houses such as Louis Vuitton, Chanel, and Charles Jourdan, others newer brands such as Donna Karan, Giorgio Armani, and Ralph Lauren, who appealed to a glossy generation of youthful consumers. This demographic now had a new moniker: *yuppie*, or young upwardly mobile professional. Brand names were the new religion for these brash city slickers, who, despite their pushy metropolitan chic, seemed to have a rather precarious personal identity predicated on aspirational lifestyle labels, bought because they reflected (or seemed to reflect) the desirable life that was being led.

With purses stuffed with credit cards, and Filofaxes at the ready, yuppies were a literal embodiment of eighties cynicism and greed, representing the cutthroat Conservatism of Margaret Thatcher in the United Kingdom and Ronald Reagan in America—both free-market economies in which only the fit survived. The "work hard, play hard" ethos assiduously promoted in this decade was satirized in *American Psycho*, Brett Easton Ellis's poisonous novel of 1991. Antihero Patrick Bateman

LEFT *In 1987, Moët & Chandon, Hennessy, and Louis Vuitton merged to form LVMH, the world's largest luxury-goods conglomerate. Subsidiaries include many manufacturers of bags, including Fendi and Donna Karan.*

RIGHT *A decadent glamour entered fashion imagery in the mid-1970s through the work of photographers Guy Bourdin and Helmut Newton. A metallic silver leather shoulder bag shimmers in this 1975 scene.*

is a psychopathic Wall Street broker who earns a fortune by day, but at night transforms into a ruthless and terrifying serial killer. In between scenes of unimaginable horror, the book is punctuated by a litany of designer brand names, in which the handbag features as a prop to display fashion savvy. For instance, after debating the merits of "a new Californian-Sicilian bistro," Bateman and friends end up at fashionable eatery Pastels and, with Bellinis in hand, point out girls in, variously,

> *… a chemise dress in double-faced wool by Calvin Klein … a wool knit dress and jacket with silk faille bonding by Geoffrey Beene … a symmetrical skirt of pleated tulle and an embroidered velvet bustier by Christian Lacroix … And a definite model type, thin, okay tits, no ass, high heels—and she's wearing a wool-crepe skirt and a wool and cashmere velour jacket and draped over her arm is a wool and cashmere velour coat, all by Louis Dell'Olio. High-heeled shoes by Susan Bennis Warren Edwards. Sunglasses by Alan Mikli. Pressed leather bag from Hermès.*[16]

One of Bateman's future victims, Bethany, wears "a silk gazar blouse and a silk satin skirt with crinoline. A Paloma Picasso hunter green suede and wrought-iron handbag sits in front of her on the table, next to a bottle of San Pellegrino water."[17] Bethany, a successful broker at Milbank Tweed, is a cool, confident executive who dares to pay the lunch bill after their date at the latest chi-chi bar, leaving Bateman reaching for his nail gun.

> *The waiter finally brings the check.*
> *"I'll pay for it," I sigh.*
> *"No," she says, opening her handbag.*
> *"I invited you."*
> *"But I have a platinum American Express card," I tell her.*
> *"But so do I," she says smiling.*
> *I pause, then watch her place the card on the tray the check came on. Violent convulsions seem close at hand if I do not get up. "The women's movement. Wow." I smile, unimpressed.*[18]

Bethany may have been a fictional character, but the stereotype of eighties woman as ball-busting executive, in control and dressed for success, did hold a grain of truth. A subtle shift in the workforce was felt, specifically in Europe and America, as more and more women began to push more confidently against the glass ceiling, seeking jobs of power and authority rather than settling for the traditional role of office secretary. In 1984, writer Pearson Philips attempted a taxonomy of the modus operandi of the female yuppie: "Suzie Yap, 29, lives alone in her house with a rare wire-haired Abyssinian cat called Purr Centage ('Cents for short'). She works for the London branch of an American Bank, is responsible for the day-to-day management of £630 millions worth of funds, and enjoys eating, squash and Kaniku (a form of mental Karate)."[19] Suzie Yap goes on to describe a typical day in which she kicks off the morning with a call to Tokyo to check the global markets, then goes off on a run, picks up the papers, and then pulls on her preplanned wardrobe: "Everything will be waiting for me, correctly co-ordinated, from shoes to silk scarf … Having arrived a certain way up the ladder I choose good quality clothes in good fabrics and up-to-date styles. I always wear the current line. It is important to look as though you know what is going on in the world around you."[20]

By 1967, Gucci successfully marketed a range of man-bags in Italy that were also sold in America with some success; author Truman Capote was an early advocate, musing, "I don't see how people can get along without some sort of little satchel."[32] British DJ Jimmy Savile had a suede patchwork bag by Maria and Stussy in which to carry his Cuban cigars, while Marnie Fogg remembers going to Italy in the early 1970s and seeing "practically every man with a small bag dangling from the wrist. They were small, black leather and zippered. Maybe it's because the culture is so macho they could get away with it. They never, ever caught on in England though."[33]

The hippie movement was a global campaign for change, supporting sexual and racial equality, an end to the Vietnam War, a more experimental attitude to living, and a break with materialism. "Dropping out" was seen as a way of expressing these alternative beliefs or expanding one's consciousness through drugs such as LSD, and with this new lifestyle came new modes of dress— kaftans, headbands, beards, and beads. Marnie Fogg remembers a defining moment in 1969 when drug culture and bag fashions collided:

I remember being at a house party held by the local "heads" with the neighbors complaining at the volume that "Hot Rats" by Frank Zappa was being played. The floorboards were literally shaking. My friend began staring fixedly at her patchwork bag as if the appliquéd rainbow was going to burst into a million stars. She began fingering the beaded tassels and continued for what seemed hours, cooing intermittently, "Man, these are so...o...o beautiful." Suddenly, to my horror, she pulled off her caftan, stuffed it inside her bag and made a dash, stark naked, to the front door. I vowed never to let her take acid again.[34]

Identifying with the marginalized was a central tenet of hippie philosophy. The patched jeans favored by hippies became the uniform of disaffected youth across the world as Western fashion was ignored in favor of a nonconformist, multicultural look. As Wilson and Taylor observe:

Ethnic fashions could be worn in solidarity with the oppressed nations of the non-Western world as students across the globe became politicized, particularly by the Vietnam War. Afghan coats embroidered on the outside and with the long wool worn as a lining; cheap Indian cotton printed full-length dresses with mirror embroidery; American Indian beaded head and fringed suede ... By 1970, home-made clothing no longer seemed an inferior substitute for ready-made clothes; on the contrary there was a positive value attached to anything handmade, even if it were only a macramé belt or choker, as a reaction against the super-shininess of PVC, the too knife-like pleats of Terylene.[35]

Northern American Indian beading and fringing appeared on bags as a form of identification with a culture that had been systematically decimated by the American behemoth. Army satchels were taken from those in control, their rabid military imperialism subverted when brandished by those who were questioning authority. Craftwork and customization won out over couture, and plastic was dumped in favor of natural materials. Bags were bigger, soft, and unstructured—tote bags made out of tapestry, furnishing fabric, or ethnic textiles bought from the local head shop. The carpet bag even made a comeback. Patchwork was particularly popular, a nostalgic revival of a traditional American folk craft in opposition to the once fashionable space-age look, which was rapidly losing its lure. Nature had won out over science; small-scale handcrafting took over in the age of the machine. Bags were no longer symbols of teenage fashionability but objects denoting empathy with a rural past destroyed by capitalist industrialization, or made by some distant tribe unsullied by modernity.

Customization was an important part of the hippie aesthetic—a visual form of freedom of speech. Political badges, sew-on patches, scrawled

As Suzie Yap clearly indicates, to successfully storm the male bastions of the City one had to dress correctly. Luckily for all those potential female executives who were sartorially insecure, a handbook was there to provide all the answers: *Women, Dress for Success*, written by fashion consultant John T. Molloy in 1980. To fit in with the male status quo, Molloy believed, women had to subtly mirror the male working wardrobe, specifically the suit. They had to "package themselves" to gain the respect of their peers, using "wardrobe engineering." He claimed that "By making adjustments in a woman's wardrobe, we can make her look more successful and better educated. We can increase her chances of success in the business world; we can increase her chances of becoming a top executive; and we can make her more attractive to various types of men."[21]

Molloy realized that as the suit signified status in business, it was the tried and trusted choice for any ambitious woman. Aspiring Suzie Yaps should wear well-tailored but unobtrusive blazers and tweeds in colors such as gray, medium-range blue, beige, deep maroon, and rust and should avoid pastels, particularly pink and pale yellow, at all costs—those colors were absurdly feminine and "un-authoritative." Bright colors were also out—too "exotic," according to Molloy. Of course, Molloy had something to say about handbags, and he was overwhelmingly negative: they were anathema to any successful woman, too traditionally associated with femininity and thus insufficiently businesslike. As he put it, "Never carry a handbag when you could carry a briefcase."[22] It was not just the bags themselves that were a problem, though, it was the way women used them, as Molloy explained: "We ran a small test to learn what female habits annoy male executives. One such trait was fumbling through their handbags when they were to pay for lunch. Men don't object to women paying; in fact some of them enjoy it. It's making such a fuss over it that seems to annoy them."[23]

F. PINET
BOND STREET, LONDON

47 NEW BOND STREET, LONDON W1. TEL: 01-629 2174

Successful women carried briefcases—women like Sigourney Weaver in the film *Working Girl* (1988), who carried a crisp attaché case, as opposed to her secretary-cum-mall chick Melanie Griffith, who carried a baggy tote. There was just one problem with Molloy's argument, though: the most powerful woman in the Western world, Margaret Thatcher, always carried a handbag—a big fat Ferragamo to boot—and she certainly had no problems in maintaining authority over male members of her cabinet.

Thatcher's bag was middle-class, durable, "good"—and it flew in the face of fashion. It was as if two decades had passed her by: no miniskirts or Indian beads for her; instead she was a marvel of meticulous fifties grooming—a clever strategy for a woman responsible for changing the face of Conservatism in the twentieth century from the party of toffs to the natural home of the ordinary working man. Thatcher's bag was nostalgic, suburban; it reflected a wholesome upbringing in the modest market town of Grantham with her grocer father, before the swinging sixties and seventies had brought about the destruction of family values and all that civilized people held dear. It was a canny move: a display of "ordinariness" by a woman who reached her position of power precisely because of radical social change (although she might have said "despite it"). As historian Wendy Webster expressed it in her illuminating study of Thatcher's rise to power:

It would have been hard to imagine an image which could have worked better to disassociate Mrs Thatcher's candidacy from notions of feminism and to counter the view that in standing for leadership of the party as a woman, she was challenging established patterns of behaviour and gender roles, and threatening the received order. The image spoke, not of disruption, but of continuity, of a reassuringly conventional rather than threatening or frightening woman, of someone who, rather than challenging her designated social role, was dedicated to its performance.[24]

Thatcher used the imagery of housewifery throughout the 1980s to illustrate her own economic policies—thrift, common sense, and efficiency—not that she had ever been much of a housewife herself. Her choice of handbag reinforced these values. Some saw beneath the surface, though, one journalist describing his prime minister as having "the porcelain prettiness of an Edwardian doll ... And the single-mindedness of a Manchester United football supporter."[25] Perhaps it is not surprising that in popular mythology Thatcher is supposed to have wielded her Ferragamo as an offensive weapon, "handbagging" members of the Opposition and the cringing, craven yes-men of her own team to get her own way, butchering her opponents with blows from her bag like a latter-day Boadicea. Today, Prime Minister Margaret Thatcher's black leather Ferragamo is firmly established as an evocative symbol of eighties Conservatism. The iconic status of her "trusty companion," as she called the much-loved accessory, was consolidated in 2000 when it sold on eBay for $150,000.

As well as the indomitable Thatcher, other powerful women were prepared to flout Molloy's advice, realizing that femininity and status were not incompatible in the workplace. Women may have entered the hierarchical office structure as diluted men in their dismal suits, but as they gained confidence, power dressing, as it began to be known, transformed businesswear into a look both brash and sexy. The office glamazon shortened the skirt of her sharply tailored suit, exaggerated its padded shoulders, intensified its color into fuchsia pink or lipstick red, added a pair of killer heels, and brandished a designer bag. Everyone wanted to look as if they had an office to go to (preferably one that they owned), and businesswomen dressed to kill, taking as their role model Joan Collins as superbitch Alexis Carrington Colby in the popular television series *Dynasty*. Conspicuous wealth was worshipped and greed was deemed good. Novelist Tom Wolfe documented this time of gross excess in his brilliant evocation of eighties New York, *The Bonfire of the Vanities*:

When Maria finally appeared [at international arrivals, Kennedy airport], she wasn't hard to spot ... She looked like something from another galaxy. She was wearing a skirt and big-shouldered jacket of a royal blue that was fashionable in France, a blue-and-white-striped silk blouse, and electric-blue lizard pumps with white calf caps on the toes. The price of the blouse and the shoes alone would have paid for the clothes on the backs of any twenty women on the floor. She walked with a nose-up sprocket-hipped model-girl gait calculated to provoke maximum envy and resentment. People were staring. Beside her marched a porter with an aluminum dolly cart heaped with luggage, a prodigious amount of it, a matched set, cream-colored leather with a chocolate trim on the edges. Vulgar, but not as vulgar as Louis Vuitton.[26]

Maria's flashy bags epitomize the new vulgarity that entered accessory design in this decade of aggressive excess. Karl Lagerfeld, who took over as Chanel's design director in 1983, expressed the aesthetic perfectly when he redesigned the classic 2.55 bag and morphed its shape into attaché dimensions to create the modern high-flying businesswoman's equivalent of the briefcase. The Chanel logo became a brashly dominant feature, madly exaggerated as a form of extremely conspicuous consumption, while the ubiquitous gilt chain was plumped out to almost rope-like proportions—all, regrettably, carried by owners without irony. Donna Karan launched a series of satellite bags, small *pochettes* that were kept by day inside a Karan-designed briefcase, to be brandished as power lunches segued into cocktail hour.

Evening bags began to spiral out of control, loaded down with baubles and beads, the more expensive the better. The most coveted were by American designer Judith Leiber, who single-handedly revived the thirties minaudière with her exquisite status bags. Although Leiber's label had

been established in 1963, it was her evening minaudières encrusted with Swarovski crystals—up to 7,000 of them, all studded by hand—that secured for her a place in the handbag hall of fame, as Anna Johnson describes:

She found her hallmark "look" by a happy accident. Although she set out to design a round-bottomed, solid metallic evening bag in the shape of a medieval coin purse (a chatelaine), her first prototype came back from Italy imperfect. To cover a patch of botched gold plating, Leiber scattered rhinestones across the bag's base. The result was the first Judith Leiber metal bag, the Chatelaine, a precursor to her most famous evening bag, the minaudiere. Inspired by the solid art deco box bags of Van Cleef and Arpels and fabricated in gold plate, the chatelaine was made for long enchanted evenings and short black cocktail dresses.[27]

Leiber's minaudières took a variety of shapes: tulips, snails, cats, and Fabergé eggs. They were luxurious collectibles for the very, very rich, a select group whose patronage was rewarded during the years of the Reagan administration. Ronald Reagan, a president "dedicated to visible wealth and an unchecked new luxury,"[28] according to cultural historian Debora Silverman, had the inimitable Nancy as his First Lady, a woman who could have been the blueprint for one of Tom Wolfe's rapacious American fashion mavens of the 1980s: Women "of a certain age, all of them skin and bones (starved to near perfection). To compensate for the concupiscence missing from their juiceless ribs and atrophied backsides, they turned to the dress designers. This season no puffs, flounces, pleats, ruffles, bibs, bows, batwings, scallops, laces, darts, or shirrs on the bias were too extreme. They were the social X-rays."[29]

Nancy Reagan hit the headlines as a fully paid-up member of what was dubbed the Shiny Set, an elite group of visibly wealthy Americans who were key customers of couture. Fellow Shinies included Lynn Wyatt and Pat Buckley, who were both socially and politically affiliated with the Republican party. The strong dollar was flashed at all the classic French ateliers as the Shiny Set romped through Paris waving their wads of hard cash. But Nancy tended to patronize the stores of Beverly Hills, favoring Gucci above all, and manager Carlo Celoni recalls closing the store to customers in 1980 so that Nancy could spend two hours picking up some free gifts:

When she came in after the presidential election, I gave her a black silk egg purse ($600), a miniature beige calf bag with bamboo handle—style 0633—the $650 one that Jackie Onassis made famous in America, so, of course, it was a favorite of Nancy's, too—plus a dressy daytime black lizard bag ($650), and a white evening bag accented with our double G ($850) to go with the white Galanos gown she planned to wear to the inaugural balls.[30]

LEFT *A Gucci clutch and purse from 1981. Logos became an overt sign of the visibly wealthy in the 1980s as the "greed is good" mentality changed the aesthetic of the handbag.*

RIGHT *Nancy Reagan's fashion consumption was legendary in eighties America. Here, she wears the uniform of the Shiny Set, a fur coat accessorized with an expensive leather clutch.*

The bags of Judith Leiber were another hit with the First Lady, especially the bejeweled minaudières, each costing thousands of dollars—the perfect evening bags to be paraded at state banquets and trips overseas. Nancy's booty cost her nothing, a fact that increasingly goaded the press and irritated the American people as public spending shrank and their tax bills grew. The sight of Mrs. Reagan brandishing Martin van Schaak bags that cost almost $42,000 was the last straw, and questions began to be asked in the Senate. Why were Nancy's bags not being declared and taxed? And why on earth did she need 12 double closets stuffed with gratis gowns from the world's greatest fashion designers? Kitty Kelley, Nancy's unofficial biographer, describes how:

After months of unrelenting criticism, the First Lady capitulated. She hoisted a white flag and announced that she would no longer amass haute couture because it was "misunderstood."

"The First Lady will discontinue accepting clothes from American designers," said her press secretary, "but she will continue to donate her own clothes to museums because she believes that the clothing of any particular era is a visual story of the people of that period."

Mrs Reagan's press secretary told reporters that the first lady had returned an expensive handbag and belt to designer Judith Leiber. The designer was surprised to receive them. The bag and belt had been sent as birthday gifts six months before. The items were accompanied by a note from Mrs Reagan, saying that she was not wearing them and felt that someone else might use them more. Leiber, noted for her jewelled gold-plated evening bags offered to send one of her trademark cat bags. "Mrs Reagan said, 'I don't like cats—I hate cats,'" Leiber recalled.[31]

The cult of visible wealth had other detractors; the Canadian poet Irving Layton was one. Layton had been gifted a Gucci bag by his in-laws after they had been on their annual trip to Europe. It was, according to the poet, too small to be useful, so he stored it away in a drawer "where over the passing weeks and months it collected ant shit and a thin layer of dust." In 1984, he retrieved the designer bag and nailed it to the house wall outside "to keep away the vampires of materialism and acquisitiveness."[32] For Layton, the bag was a talisman that served "as a constant reminder of how easy it is to slide into the inferno of lovelessness, pride, and greed, and of the bloated soul-less faces one encounters there." Hanging on the wall like a "Transylvanian bat," the bag served to remind the poet that designer labels were pure evil with the potential to open up cracks "in the soul of every man and woman … just a small hairline crack and the devil walks in."[33]

Designer bags were seen as an unnecessary encumbrance on the journey of the spirit, on which many were preparing to embark by the early 1990s. A New Age was looming. Being eco-friendly was the way to save the world from the destruction wrought by rampant materialism; the green consumer needed to find a new, more understated way of revealing her fashion credentials.

SIX

ARM CANDY

Q. What makes a good bag?

A. You gotta have it or you'll die!

TOM FORD AT GUCCI[1]

In 1985, Miuccia Prada constructed an androgynous, ascetic backpack out of black *pocono* nylon, a material manufactured by a parachute company. This object of absolute discretion became the bag that defined the 1990s, the complete antithesis of the flamboyant, logo-laden bags of the previous decade. The eighties trappings of luxurious excess were anathema in a new decade that was calling for a global change in consciousness—spirituality, sensitivity, and eco-awareness rather than shopping and fucking—and a new vocabulary of design was therefore needed. The Prada backpack led the way: An *oggetti di lusso*, or luxury item, but one deliberately difficult to decipher, this was a coolly ironic accessory that broke the rules of conspicuous consumption with its subtle understatement—for where were the usual brassy gilt logos; the flashy fabrics; the leather, fur, and feathers?

The iconic Prada backpack was modernist, lightweight, fashioned out of cheap industrial material, stamped with a diminutive logo, and presented in austere graphic black. This was antifashion *in extremis*, but, luckily for the lifestyle consumer, reassuringly expensive enough to separate the fashion cognoscenti from the witless hordes—a bag for the "connoisseur rather than the consumer,"[2] as Miuccia explained. Fashion journalist Lisa Armstrong attempted to enlighten her bemused audience about this new style in an article for British *Vogue* in 1995: "Eighties snobbery may have been simplistic, but … it was democratic, easily grasped by everyone. This new version, by contrast, has taken to its heart a completely different system of status symbols that, far from being recognized from the other end of Bond Street, couldn't be identified from next door."[3]

If this was bag as lifestyle choice, what sort of lifestyle did it signify for the nineties consumer? The answer was minimalist—the designer's response to environmental disaster, world recession, and global poverty. Minimalism was a canny way of selling fashion, that medium that operates on the basis of

LEFT *A satchel from leather goods specialist Nazareno Gabrielli of Tolentino, Italy. In the early 1990s, under the design directorship of Daniela Puppa, minimalism dominated.*

BELOW *In 1993, husband and wife team Andy and Kate Spade set up Kate Spade, New York, specializing in handbags that were simply constructed, stylish, and practical. The nylon tote bag is one of the most successful bag designs of all time.*

novelty for novelty's sake, whose seasonal changes are designed to make perfectly wearable clothes outmoded. Such an ethos was totally unacceptable in a climate of New Age "green-ness" and the mania for recycling. Minimalism's new take on modernism was the perfect way to make women appear both chic and environmentally aware, and the Prada backpack was a textbook example of such cutting-edge aesthetics. The bag became fashion's equivalent of downsizing: A hands-free option for the city nomad; an example of stealth wealth in the midst of a culture suffering from pre-millennium tension; the bag equivalent of the waif, the new breed of model cantering down the catwalk and appearing in Calvin Klein's grungy ads in the skinny shape of Kate Moss. This was a bag fit for a more sober world, where "ostentation is not simply unaffordable but passé," as journalist William Langley put it.[4]

The success of the Prada backpack encouraged other designers—Chanel, Hermès, Louis Vuitton, and Donna Karan to name but a few—to follow suit with their own versions. And this look of nineties restraint spread to other bags, with names such as Loewe, Longchamps, Osprey, Bill Amberg, and Calvin Klein concentrating on form and structure rather than applied decoration and obvious logos. Kate Spade's no-nonsense totes struck a chord with thousands of American women, while the fanny pack, or bum bag, was another popular hands-free alternative.

Minimalism wasn't *really* antifashion, however; it was just a new vocabulary with which the consumer had to get to grips. Its plainness was deceptive and the mask of puritan abstinence it presented slipped when one looked at the price tag. But for most of the population, Prada poverty-chic was indistinguishable from the real thing, making the style perfect for the increasingly violent city streets. Flagrant displays of wealth were imprudent in the 1990s. Minimalism was the safer option: It granted fashion cachet to those in the know, yet at the same time a certain degree of anonymity to the wearer, who stood less chance of getting mugged. Fashion could be used as a kind of protective screening device, and this idea took a more obviously military turn as the decade progressed and the Gulf War, terrorist attacks, and fear of unchecked viruses, such as Ebola and MRSA, took their toll on the psychological health of the Western world.

As minimalism segued into martial law, bags began to hug the body as fashionable safety shields, many worn slung across the torso to deter the passing pickpocket. The concept was more fully explored in the work of Vexed Generation, a design duo comprising Adam Thorpe and Joe Hunter established in 1994. Their clothing designs were for the postnuclear urban environment: "Design solutions for contemporary living,"[5] as they described them, which used performance fabrics such as the rather brutally named ballistic nylon; anti-bacterial fire-retardant fleece; and Kevlar, a light but deceptively strong aramid fiber used for "soft" armor such as bulletproof vests. Vexed Generation's products perfectly suited these hard times, addressing pressing issues such as air pollution, urban surveillance, and the threat of terrorist attack—albeit in a somewhat symbolic way.

By the early 2000s, the designers, together with the University of the Arts, London, began to develop a range of unisex bags, "performance designed to combat crime," under the brand name Karrysafe. Conceived to "deter the most common techniques of street criminals: dipping, grabbing, lifting and slashing," the bags were also designed with fashion in mind, embodying the values of Vexed Generation's "stealth utility." Designs included the Scroll Top shoulder bag in "high tenacity Corura nylon with a reinforced nylon webbing strap and Velcro closure," and the Body Safe, "a lingerie-style stealth belt" designed to hold a cell phone in the waistband of a pair of jeans.[6] This modern version of the traditional bag-as-pocket was essentially a black mesh belt with separate compartments for a cell phone, purse, and keys. The belt was then worn just under the

waistband of a pair of hipster jeans, in imitation of black lacy underwear that appeared to have ridden up rather erotically. The connection with lingerie was reinforced with the belt's fastenings, which were designed to resemble the hooks of a bra.

Survivalist sentiment and the urge for self-protection informed global fashion to such an extent that by the early 2000s, urban armies could be seen on every main street in every main city across the world. Young adults draped in camouflage, cargo pants, and parkas carried bags that looked like pieces of military equipment engineered ergonomically to fit the body. Backpacks sat flat against the body in techno fabrics such as neoprene; bags covered the torso like safety vests and many had names that spoke of war, including the Fiorucci Urban Camo Bag and Yuk Pak's Wrap Holster. Fashion historians Steele and Borelli described this popular style in 1999: "In contrast to the fourteen-carat gold alloy hardware used by Chanel … utility bags feature more industrial materials. These include buckles of plated steel, the kind of webbing used in seatbelts, 3M reflective tape, fishing zippers, nylon mesh, and lots of Velcro for easy access to multiple pockets and flaps." The actual functionality of the "stealth utility" aesthetic was debatable, though, as Steele and Borelli went on to observe:

> *A vest bag, viewed flat, or a small waist pack laid out on a table is a perfect example of minimalist chic – elegant, flat, and androgynous. But although sleek when empty, these bags often look fat and lumpy when filled with more than a credit card. This kangaroo aesthetic is not conventionally attractive, since vest bags and fanny packs conceal the sexually diamorphic curves of the female figure.[7]*

By 1999 *Vogue* was moved to comment, "Could the handbag, so aloof and detached, soon be obsolete?"[8] Chanel certainly didn't think so: Only the year before, the prestigious atelier had invested thousands of dollars launching its new utility-style version of the classic 2.55, the 2005, the first of its

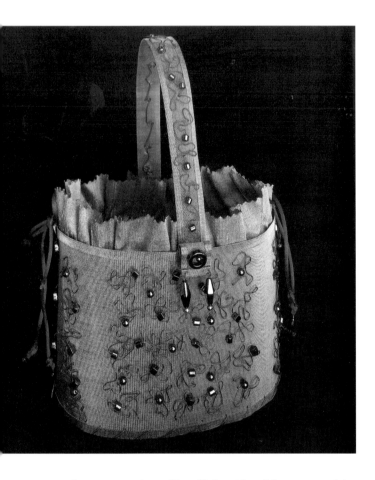

"next generation of bags." The title of the new model was a little complicated—the *2* indicated that the bag was launched two years before the millennium, the *00* referred to the international calling code, and the *5* was Coco's lucky number, as in Chanel No. 5. This was a smooth, sophisticated stealth bomber of a bag, "bio-designed" by Karl Lagerfeld in what he called "a completely new shape … body-friendly." He added: "The inside is all very refined with tons of details that make it very expensive."[9] The sleek biomorphic curves were constructed out of a frame of injection-molded polyethylene, creating an appropriately ergonomic look that screamed nineties minimalism—but unfortunately made the bag look uncannily like a piece of luggage by Samsonite. So as not to put off his conservative clientele, Lagerfeld insisted that the frame be covered with rather traditional tweed, jersey, or leather to match the owner's Chanel suit; retained a clear logo in the form of two metal discs on each side of the bag's body; and in interviews always emphasized the high price of such an exclusive item. Lagerfeld hoped to have created a new classic, but in essence the 2005 was a bizarre hybrid—it seemed to be desperately referencing the vogue for minimalist utility while at the same time attempting to maintain Chanel's image of pure luxury. Not surprisingly, this was not one of the greatest aesthetic successes in handbag history.

There was another strategy that could be adopted in the midst of such style wars: The bag could gain spiritual status if presented as an objet d'art. Violette Nozieres and Nathalie Hambro were the first of this new breed, presenting themselves as designers who produced artworks—"but not at the expense of utility,"[10] Hambro hastily commented, cleverly sidestepping any concerns that her bags may be art for art's sake. Using what she called "humble materials," such as industrial felt, nylon, and horsehair, Hambro meticulously created a series of limited-edition, hand-finished bags in 1997. Their function was to be as much an object of aesthetic contemplation as something to cart stuff around in— tellingly, they often ended up in museum collections. Hambro was an artist creating sculptures for specialist collectors with exquisite taste rather than for shallow fashionistas, wooing them with her intellectual aphorisms such as, "I find developing new techniques rewarding and I believe in the aesthetic philosophy which says that everything could and should be made beautiful, creating a value system in which all objects large or small, expensive or cheap are of real value," and "the little imperfections of a handmade bag add a certain charm that can't be found in the uniformity of a manufactured one."[11]

Hambro's approach was cultured: small scale in operation, leaving the artist time and space to contemplate each object as it was lovingly crafted. But could this refined methodology work in the global marketplace, where the big fashion houses dealt in thousands of units worth millions of dollars? Surprisingly, yes. Hambro went on to work for Balmain, and the "craft" aesthetic was used very successfully to market (rather than manufacture) the first true It bag: the Fendi Baguette.

Realizing that fashion was experiencing only a momentary seizure in its renunciation of status dressing, and that the rich could bear "stealth utility" only for so long, Fendi floated the Baguette in 1997. It became one of the most successful bags of all time.

LEFT *The Fendi Baguette shape was a perfect example of ergonomics, fitting snugly beneath a woman's arm like the eponymous bread stick after which it was named. It spawned a host of imitators.*

RIGHT *Baguettes came in an astonishing array of colors, beading, fur, and feathers. Luxury, yet bohemian, they were instantly recognizable by the Fendi logo clasp.*

The Baguette was the bag for the *haut* hippie, a newly spiritually and artistically aware woman who shopped at Voyage and lived in Notting Hill or Greenwich Village. Cleverly conflating the idea of the bag as an exquisite one-off art object with the new luxury that was beginning to infiltrate high fashion of the new millennium, Silvia Venturini produced thousands of Baguette bags in 600 different choices of luxurious materials and luscious colorways, its interlocking double-F logo forming the clasp, which was heavily embellished with crystal, paillette sequins, and beads.

Fendi's dated eighties look was salvaged with Venturini's "maximalist" bag. It was what every design house desired by the early 2000s: an instant classic, particularly when clutched under the arm of high-octane stars such as Madonna and Naomi Campbell. This small *pochette* could be purchased in silk velvet, fur, snakeskin, crocodile, woven raffia, or printed pony and was named the Baguette because its short strap meant it sat under the arm like a loaf of French bread, an elite yet bohemian accessory that became folk costume for the super-rich. Luxurious beadwork made global references to appeal to the "ethical" consumer by using North American Indian and Aztec motifs, which were in turn accented with materials that were pure old-school glamour—hot-pink snakeskin, Swarovski crystals, and silver and gold distressed sequins. "Homespun" craft techniques such as Indian mirror work, usually seen only on imported ethnic duds, appeared on the outside of the Baguette, which then flashed a wild citrus python lining or apple green satin when opened. Classic tartan mohair or workaday denim was transformed with red sequins and gold beads as tradition was coupled with sex appeal. The bag sold by the truckload, even though one well-known fashion editor had to carry a Safeway shopping bag to supplement the Baguette's lack of storage space—when pressed, she claimed she was making an ironic gesture.

In fiction, a Fendi creation was sported by another fashion editor, this one rather less respectful of such a desirable (and expensive) object, almost as if by treating a beautiful bag with disdain she could demonstrate her power, wealth, and fashion status. In Lauren Weisberger's best-selling novel *The Devil Wears Prada* (2003), fashion editor and boss-from-hell Miranda cares little for her Fendi, as noted with mounting incredulity by her newly appointed fashion assistant Andrea:

It was a one-of-a-kind tote that had been hand-beaded in an elaborate crystal design just for Miranda from Silvia Venturini Fendi, as a thank-you for all of her support, and one of the fashion assistants had put its value at just under ten grand. But I noticed today that one of the skinny leather handles had broken loose yet again, even though the accessories department had returned it to Fendi for hand-stitching two dozen times already. It was intended to hold a delicate ladies' wallet, perhaps accompanied by a pair of sunglasses or maybe, if absolutely necessary, a small cell phone. Miranda didn't really care about that. She had currently crammed in an extra-large bottle of Bulgari perfume, a sandal with a broken heel, the blotter-sized Hermès daily planner that weighed more than an entire laptop, an oversized spiked dog collar that either belonged to Madeleine or was for an upcoming fashion shoot and the Book ... I would have hocked a bag worth ten thousand dollars and paid my rent for a year, but Miranda preferred to use it as a trash receptacle.[12]

All of a sudden, luxury was being lauded as nothing to be ashamed of, reaching a spectacular crescendo with the fashion shows of John Galliano at Dior and Alexander McQueen for Givenchy in the 1990s that cost upward of $2 million to stage. Young cutting-edge designers were brought in to revamp old brands: Tom Ford for Gucci in 1990, Marc Jacobs for Louis Vuitton in 1997, and Belgian deconstructionist Martin Margiela for Hermès in 1998—and It bag followed It bag. Designer bags were a license for labels to print money. The litany of must-haves began with the Lady Dior of 1994, sported by Princess Diana herself, which was all dangling gold letter charms and "the leather equivalent of a yapping Chihuahua,"[13] as journalist Mimi Spencer described it in 1997, the year 140,000 were sold at $1,200 each. Successors included the Vuitton Graffiti (1999) by underground artist turned catwalk designer Stephen Sprouse, a bag that transposed the raw power of a spray-painted subway wall onto the hide of a luxury calfskin bag; the Prada bowling bag, utility dressed to thrill in black ostrich skin (2000); and the Murakami Monogram (2002), a quirky anime version of the classic Vuitton canvas for LV's loyal Japanese customers. Tom Ford updated Gucci's signature bamboo handles, abstracted its metal snaffles, and fixed them onto sensuous bags of python, fur, and metallic leather. Logos were cool again.

With bags now so successful, and generating so much income, the next step was to make them seasonal, following the established patterns of fashionable dress. This was a revolutionary idea, completely changing the culture of the designer bag, which formerly operated on establishing one or two hits each decade—the logo-ed Gucci in the 1970s, for instance, or the eighties revamp of the Chanel 2.55. Designers now began to vie with one another to create the definitive (and most lucrative) bag, parading it on the catwalk as the focal point of each collection. At the shows for Spring/Summer 2006, for instance, all eyes at Prada were on the colossal

LEFT *Supermodel and style icon Kate Moss kick-started many an It bag trend. Here she carries a black leather Balenciaga bag designed by Nicholas Ghesquiere.*

BELOW *The Mulberry Araline by Stuart Vevers is a soft nappa leather bag with less over-styled detailing than most. The handle is in the form of a woven leather rope with large tassels on each end.*

Journalist Zoe Williams was particularly caustic about this so-called celebrity endorsement in 2006 in an article entitled, "To them, free. To you, £595."

I bring you the news of the It bag of the summer. "The Emmy, £595, Mulberry's bag of the season, which already has a celebrity following that includes Jennifer Aniston …" It would be unfair to go on about which paper that came from, since you could have read the same in any broadsheet or tabloid, whether leftist or rightist – in fact any written medium at all – in this country, in this century. Every part of the statement is true: this bag exists, and it has been named the Emmy. Jennifer Aniston is a celebrity … The statement, overall, however, is a lie – everybody knows how this stuff works. Hypothetical company sends one bag to a whole heap of celebrities; maybe they concentrate on the ones who go to the most parties, or maybe they just send out hundreds. I don't know. Hypothetical celebrity, in order to "endorse" this product, has to do no more than transfer wallet, drugs and haemorrhoid cream from old handbag, which they were also sent free, to this new handbag, and then leave the house with it at once … And yet it's all delivered – Sarah Jessica Parker swears by this, Keira Knightley can't live without that – as if it might have some truth or meaning. There is no other branch of journalism in which the PR is propagated so unquestioningly … You might think, well, it's only a trivial handbag. It's not about the bags, it's about the peddling of bilge. Why aren't people more embarrassed?[14]

bubblegum-pink wheeled luggage that the models were artlessly trundling down the catwalk.

With new versions coming out for each season, a bag could seem desperately old-fashioned after only one or two turns around the block, and could potentially make a fashionable woman a laughing stock among her peers—or so designers hoped. The other marketing ploy that quickly became established practice in the 2000s was *seeding*, the name given to the process by which a fashion house's PR department gives away free bags to the hottest celebrity of the moment with the hope that they will be photographed brandishing it at some swanky event. It has been said that between 2005 and 2006, Sienna Miller received almost 30 bags a month, some worth as much as $60,000.

But the strategies for pushing the seasonal bag appeared to be working. By 2006, sales of bags were growing at twice the rate of clothes; journalist Alice Fisher wrote, "the current level of obsession with this sector of the accessories market is unprecedented."[15] And obsession it was: A 2006 marketing report by Mintel claimed that British women spent £350 million a year on bags, and sales were up by a massive 146% in five years.

Prices escalated but still failed to stem the demand; what were credit cards for anyway? Stuart Vevers, the most successful bag designer of the 2000s having created a series of It bags for Vuitton, Bottega Veneta, Givenchy, and Mulberry, commented in 2006, "Every time I think there's a limit within accessories or handbags, we go through another one. I remember when handbags were £500, and I thought no one would ever go above that. Now they're well over £1,000 and there's no sign of stopping." [16]

The obsession with the bag of the season was also fuelled by its unavailability. Kate Moss was always able to get her hands on the latest luxury

bag—a Balenciaga Lariat, a Fendi Spy—but for the Average Joe it was well nigh impossible. One had to join the waiting list, rumored to be up to three years long for a high-status bag like the Hermès Birkin. As the anonymous designer in *Fashion Babylon* (2006), Imogen Edwards-Jones's exposé of the industry, explained:

Once your bag is so sought after that there's a waiting list, you can smile all the way to the bank. Buyers go crazy for them. I remember Matches had Chloe Paddington bag evenings where only the most loyal customer was allowed to purchase the bag under the counter, like some very special blend of fashion crack cocaine. It sold out worldwide without ever making it to the shop floor. A couple of seasons ago Luella Bartley managed to clean up with her Gisele handbag. Fendi has recently closed the waiting list on its £1,010 B Bag with new stock not expected until some time next year. [17]

In 2005, Alexander McQueen stirred up customer demand to fever pitch when he announced the launch of his new bag, the Novak, named after Kim Novak, the legendary blonde actress who starred in Alfred Hitchcock's 1958 masterpiece *Vertigo* as a chic, buttoned-up, yet doomed blonde who falls to her death from a bell tower in the final scenes. McQueen took Novak's structured fifties look as inspiration for a deliberately "uptight" bag in shiny nappa leather that provided a dramatic contrast to the slouchy, squishy qualities of the most popular designer bags, such as the best-selling Yves Saint Laurent Muse or the Chloe Betty. After announcing that the bag was a limited edition and that only 200 were ever to be produced, starting at £550 and rising to a whopping £6,000 for the deluxe crocodile version, the bag became the ultimate fashion trophy, selling out before it even hit the waiting list.

The Novak's lack of ornament was the exception to the rule, as the pared-down 2000s silhouette and

the obsession with overly slender bodies made the bag the only place where decoration could rage rampantly without ruining the lines of a pair of skinny jeans and a tube top. Bags became bigger and bigger, outlandishly so, as the ideal fashion body shrank to the proportions of an anorexic. Skinny celebrities were dwarfed by their overdesigned status bags that seemed to feed off them like sinister succubi, symbols of success that appeared to be taking on a life of their own, the more so when they were given female names. New best friends included Roxanne and Emmy by Mulberry, Gisele and Joni by Luella Bartley and the Chloe Gladys.

The cute names disguised the fact that this was corporate conformist fashion produced by huge conglomerations such as LVMH (Louis Vuitton Moet Hennessy), which owned most of the world's prominent luxury brands, including Chloe, Pucci, Louis Vuitton, Celine, Marc Jacobs, Fendi, Givenchy, and Donna Karan, and the Gucci Group, which controlled Stella McCartney, Alexander McQueen, Yves Saint Laurent, Bottega Veneta, Balenciaga, Sergio Rossi, and, of course, Gucci. Bags sent the profits of these companies into the stratosphere. In 2005, Louis Vuitton made billions of dollars, of which

only 10% was from clothing—the rest came from accessories. Even smaller concerns such as Anya Hindmarch were going places: In 2006 she sold a stake in her bag business to Kelso Place Asset Management, a private equity group, in a deal that valued the company at £20 million.

However, the luxury handbag was no longer the preserve of the elite or the moneyed celebrity as more and more ordinary women spent extravagant sums on the must-have bag of the season. The routine use of the epithet *must-have* was another clever marketing ploy routinely used by the fashion press, whose livelihood depended on the advertising revenue generated by the big fashion names. When a bag was deemed a must-have (like bread or water), the consumer's sense of responsibility disappeared and the need for the right bag became a visceral rather than considered purchase—"I want" was made to feel like "I need." According to cultural critic Bryan Appleyard, it is "a brilliant phrase that sums up the peculiar will to subjugation involved in the pursuit of fashion and the phenomenal success of designers in blinding their customers to the absolute futility of the products. Fashion falls down dead the moment a woman goes out to buy a bag solely because her old one has worn out."[18]

For Appleyard, the monstrous bag of the 2000s was "simply horrible": another example of fashion as purveyor of the emperor's new clothes and an example of the prevailing mood in contemporary culture that he dubs "desperatism." He claimed that consumers become totally panic-stricken when presented with the alarming number of styles in our postmodern culture—organic, distressed rusticity, resurgent modernism, new vintage, and so on, leading to a situation in which insecure consumers grab the objects with the highest price tag and the flashiest aesthetics, because "we're worth it." The bags that literally thousands of women were pursuing, desperate to be a celebrity in their own lunchtime, were described with much vituperation:

LEFT *Gianfranco Ferré, acclaimed for his designs of flamboyant luxury, shows the biggest bag of 2005. A complicated mix of macramé and leopard skin, the bag, which was inspired by the rain forest, cut a bizarre silhouette on the catwalk.*

RIGHT *Kate Moss starred in Longchamp's bag campaign of 2007, her naked body suggesting that clothes had become redundant—it was all about the It bag.*

The clutch version of the Fendi Spy Bag, with its sinister frill, looks like a diseased organ or rotting ravioli, and both the standard Spy and the Chloe Paddington look so much like scrotums that even a plain-speaking Englishman would want to call them "purses" … excessive straps hint at what is really going on here: the debauching of functionality into pure ornament. Bags, unlike say necklaces, are necessary. Thanks to mobiles, PDAs and iPods, women carry even more around with them than they used to. So we get the bulging scrotum and the big-pocket effects – the two most common themes in high-style handbag design. But even more typical is the way the presence of these apparently functional attributes is wildly exaggerated. Bags now have colossal buckles and elaborate closures … they are pure decoration. They scream "I am a useful bag" so loudly that, plainly, they are not.[19]

Appleyard's disquiet notwithstanding, the must-have bag, despite its prohibitive price, has become a true mass-market fashion object: One size fits all,

and anyone with the right amount of disposable income or a purse full of store credit cards can buy into the magic of a brand. Taste depends on having access to money (there is no such thing as a vulgar bag anymore) and while this democratization appears more egalitarian, it has enticed those with the least into massive amounts of debt. As Stuart Vevers comments:

A few years ago, designer or luxury goods were only for the elite, but now I get on the bus in Hackney and see ladies with genuine Mulberry bags that I know cost £600. Five years ago, people used to have high-street outfits and high-street bags; now they have high-street outfits but designer bags and shoes. The industry is huge, and there's no going back once people have got used to the quality.[20]

Women are now prepared to spend more on a bag than on a car or foreign vacation—and it has to be obvious to the naked eye that they've done it. Subtlety is not the way forward in the desperate twenty-first century.

So Louis Vuitton smothers its enormous black-leather and leopard-skin bags in chains; Prada invents a new piece of jewelry—the handbag charm; and Marc Jacobs's Stam has a chunky gilt chain hanging from its padded black leather body, which, like Lanvin's shiny black patent leather Merlin, would look more at home in a fetishist's dungeon. Overtly sexual bags seem to be suggesting that as women are erasing all of the erotic attributes of their body, including curves and pubic hair, it is the bag that seduces rather than the woman herself. Bags are studded, padlocked, and cuffed, and design motifs are described as *hardware*, the terminology of weaponry—an expression of our darker times, perhaps. The only remaining faux pas is to carry an obvious fake—that's what now separates the wheat from the chaff.

The embarrassment of owning a fake became the narrative thrust of an episode of *Sex and the City*, supposedly a look at the modern sexual mores of

LONGCHAMP
PARIS

LEFT *In* Sex and the City, *the popular TV series from HBO, Sarah Jessica Parker posed with a roll-call of bags, including this plush striped-velvet vintage vanity case by Roberta de Camerino.*

New York women but simultaneously a platform for advertising luxury items, thanks to stylist Patricia Field. Timmy Wood's Secretariat horse-head handbag, for instance, was glimpsed only momentarily on Carrie's shoulder, but the day after the show was aired the design duo was swamped with a thousand orders.

Sex and the City was the first television series to have its own fashion credits, which suggested that alongside the four main players—Carrie, Charlotte, Miranda, and Samantha—fashion was an equal, if silent, character. Episode 44 in Season 3 could have been sponsored by Fendi as it featured so many Baguettes—in gold, purple sequins, white diamond, and brown snake—together with a pink suede Givenchy, silver Carlos Falchi, pink corduroy Dolce & Gabbana, and a mini Louis Vuitton clutch.

The predominance of rather predictable designer bags in *Sex and the City* begged the question: Was there *any* room for quirkiness in twenty-first-century handbag design? One designer who has made the whimsical fashionable again is Lulu Guinness, whose delicious bags assume the shapes of buildings, fans, and floral baskets such as the Picnic Rose—bags that are the ultimate icebreaker at any smart soirée. As Guinness says, "If you place them on a table at an event where you don't know anyone, they almost defy people not to talk to you."[21] The Guinness brand is redolent of a cosy Englishness—all cream teas in the rectory—which is then imbued with a sense of the surreal; in particular she acknowledges her debt to the sublime Elsa Schiaparelli and Salvador Dalí, whose lip motif she converted into a red satin lip bag accented with Swarovski crystals.

Guinness bags are embroidered canvas or black satin embellished with butterflies, stiletto heels, the Queen's silhouetted head, or the Union Jack, and have evocative titles such as Stop and Smell the Roses or Friendship, Love and Truth, many of them tapping into a fantasy fifties glamour with a hint of burlesque that is rather more charming than the

LEFT *A lipstick-red surrealist bag by Lulu Guinness inspired by the famous sofa of the 1930s designed by maverick artist Salvador Dalí in the shape of Mae West's lips.*

RIGHT *Lulu Guinness's bags are witty trompe l'oeil fantasies—charming rather than oversized status symbols. Guinness spearheaded the revival of the small evening bag with designs such as this black-and-red satin posy holder.*

modern-day bump and grind version. Bags like these are avidly collected by women who have a similar fashion sensibility. Jan Birks, editor-in-chief of the *Erotic Review*, is one, a latter-day Ava Gardner who adores Lulu Guinness handbags "because they are retro, witty, and tell a story."

You can tell she embraces the play of vintage fashion. The fans and chocolate-box designs have a real sense of humor, and a new Guinness collection never ceases to surprise or delight me. When I turn up to interview people with my Lulu Guinness handbag covered in Dalmatians instead of a boxy boring briefcase, people know the experience is going to be fun! I think women who wear them are individuals, rebels even, who appreciate old-fashioned glamour, and at same time, refuse to be preached to by the dictates of the fashion industry![22]

Elsewhere, Jan Haedrich of the label My Flat in London uses a fly motif on bizarre prom bags with huge ribbon corsages, or handbags that picture pink poodles; Philip Treacy revitalizes the pop-art prints of Andy Warhol in his engineered clutches and printed canvas bucket bags. Meanwhile, Irish architect turned accessory designer Pauric Sweeney has unleashed another generation's attempt at the Holy Grail of accessory design, the man-bag. Here we have the one as yet untapped market that has design houses rubbing their hands with glee. If men carried bags, accessories revenue would be doubled, or so the logic goes.

In 2006, many designers—Prada, Gucci and Mulberry, to name but a few—began trying to reel the male consumer in. It was an uphill struggle, as it had been in the past, and not helped by media representations of men with bags as objects of ridicule. In 1999, for instance, an episode of *Friends* had featured Joey falling in love with a man-bag and losing out at an audition because he refused to let it out of his sight. In the same year, the Reverend Jerry Falwell, a spokesman for America's moral majority,

caused a furor when he suggested that Tinky Winky, one of the characters in the *Teletubbies*, might encourage gay tendencies in infants because he carried a ladies' bag.

Change was afoot, though, and, as in the early 1970s, the increasingly etiolated silhouette for men, as popularized by the designs of Hedi Slimane for Dior Homme and the skinny jeans worn by members of the newly resurgent indie music scene, made bulging pockets a thing of the past; as one journalist commented, "You'll look like a sack of potatoes within a week." David Beckham, always at the forefront of any fashion trend, was spotted out and about with a Louis Vuitton Monogram canvas clutch under his arm, and Jude Law and Jared Leto followed suit. In summer 2006, English journalist Patrick Barkham observed the man-bag beginning to take off:

It is diminutive, made from white leather and has a short brown strap. And it bobs coquettishly off the left shoulder of a man. A manly man, too, in a suit, who looks like he means business. Here's another: green leather, tucked under the arm of a trendy-looking student. A middle-aged man carries one at his side. It is square and black, but too small to be a briefcase. And there is a male tourist, sporting a beautiful soft leather-pouchy-looking thing. The scene in London is swinging, man. Swinging with man bags.[23]

The most successful man-bags had a hunting, shooting, and fishing quality to them that spoke of function rather than the trivialities of fashion—they should seem to be born of tradition rather than the effete whims of a designer. In a man's world, a designer object was acceptable if it could be categorized as hardware: laptops, MP3 players, and sports cars could be designed, but bags could not—that was one step too far into female culture. Bags had to appear to be of bucolic origin in order to be acceptable, harking back to the pursuits indulged in when men were rugged and practical.

LEFT In the 2000s, Mulberry were prepared to go into territory where no bag designer had been since the 1970s—the man-bag. The Alfie was unremarkable for its gender politics—utilitarian and functional.

RIGHT Burberry's campaigns featured man-bags that were discreet and unthreatening and made not-so-subtle references to country pursuits. This example seems more suited to carrying fish bait than a wallet.

"Eeew, what's that?"

"Oh, that's my new manbag. Do you like it?"

"Your new what?"

"Manbag. Marvellous invention. You can keep all your stuff in it, see. Keys, wallet, Polo mints, camera, fags, small bits of paper with mysterious phone numbers on them. I can't imagine why I didn't get one sooner."

"Isn't it a bit effeminate?"

"I don't think it's effeminate at all. Actually, I think only real men can carry off manbags. Look at Becks [David Beckham]: hair like a girl, more bling than a Harlem lap dancer, altogether as camp as Christmas – but no one doubts he's got balls."

"Not to mention a lovely Louis Vuitton bag to keep them in …"[24]

The names of man-bags were butch, too: Mulberry's Alfie in buffalo hide and canvas channeled a sixties Michael Caine in the film of the same name, a charismatic maverick sleeping his way around London in the Swinging Sixties; other alpha-male designs included the Seth and the Sidney. Pauric Sweeney's bags "for the modern gentleman," as he describes them, are tailored, as in the manner of Savile Row suits, in ebony, caramel, and white snakeskin and in classic shapes such as doctors' bags and duffels.

Messenger bags enjoyed a brief vogue, originating with motorcycle couriers and then copied by Fendi, Gucci, and Prada as a sophisticated alternative to the briefcase or rucksack. In 2006, Mulberry reported a 64% increase in the sales of men's accessories after their bags were seen on the arms of Tom Hanks and Mick Jagger. And even the most domestic bag of all, the tote, was rebranded as masculine rather than an accessory purely for the domestic goddess or housewife when Marc Jacobs covered one with a photograph of Al Gore after his starring role in the eco-documentary *An Inconvenient Truth* (2006), together with the slogan "Give 'Em Hell, Al."

Some have been less convinced by the possibilities of the man-bag, however, including the (London) *Times* newspaper, which ran a fantasy conversation between a man and his appalled wife in 2006.

In the first decade of the new millennium, the bag has never been more popular, and one of the most debated of cultural artifacts is in an almost unassailable position in fashion culture. Clothes on the catwalk now regularly take second place to this most fascinating of accessories, and advertising campaigns feature close-ups of skin, straps, and stitching in fetishistic detail, as a kind of alternative pornography for women to lust over. Unlike catwalk clothes, bags fit all—anyone from the sought-after size 0 to sizes 18 and upward can wear them, which is perhaps why in these body-obsessed times they are collected and brandished obsessively and without thought of cost.

For more than two centuries, bags have been preoccupying women and perplexing men, magical products of female culture that resound with meaning while remaining mysterious objects of desire. At one time hidden away beneath the folds of a petticoat, bags by the twentieth century had become as visible on the streets as the women carrying them, and they continued to evolve, embodying the zeitgeist, shape-shifting to reflect each decade's desires. Today, bags remain the most vital of accessories, the territory of women, albeit slowly being invaded by men, and still emotional baggage of the most evocative kind.

NOTES

A HISTORY OF BAGS

1 Louis Aragon, *Residential Quarters* (1936), quoted in Farid Chenoune, *Carried Away: All About Bags*. New York: The Vendome Press, 2005, p. 21.

2 Chenoune, p. 21.

THE BIRTH OF THE BAG

1 Anna Johnson, *Handbags: The Power of the Purse*. New York: Workman Publishing, 2002, p. xx.

2 Vanda Foster, *Bags and Purses*. London: Batsford, 1982, p. 12.

3 C. Willet and P. Cunnington, *Handbook of English Costume in the Eighteenth Century*. London: Faber and Faber, 1972, p. 339.

4 Johnson, p. xxiii.

5 Diary of William Taylor, quoted in Colin McDowell, *The Literary Companion to Fashion*. London: Sinclair–Stevenson, 1995, p. 428.

6 Aileen Ribeiro, *Dress and Morality*. New York: Holmes and Meier, 1986, p. 124.

7 Claire Wilcox, *Bags*. London: V&A Publications, 1999, p. 52.

8 The Williamsburg Garden Club, *A Williamsburg Scrapbook*. Richmond, Virginia: The Dietz Printing Co., 1937, p. 92.

9 Alison Lurie, *The Language of Clothes*. London: Hamlyn, 1983, p. 242.

10 Leo Tolstoy, *Anna Karenina* (1875), www.literature.org.

11 Alison Uttley, *Ambush of Young Days* (1937), quoted in McDowell, p. 40.

12 Penny Sparke, *As Long As It's Pink: The Sexual Politics of Taste*. London: Pandora, 1995, p. 110.

13 Leonore Davidoff and Catherine Hall, *Family Fortunes: Men and Women of the English Middle Class 1780–1850*. London: Routledge, 1997, p. 414.

14 Susan Brownmiller, *Femininity*. London: Hamish Hamilton, 1984, p. 199.

15 Davidoff and Hall, p. 413.

16 Foster, p. 50.

17 Jules Verne, *Around the World in Eighty Days* (1873), quoted in Paul-Gerard Pasols, *Louis Vuitton: The Birth of Modern Luxury*. New York: Harry N. Abrams, 2005, p. 64.

18 John T. Humphrey, "Useful Bags and How to Make Them," *Scientific American Supplement*, No. 561, October 2, 1886.

19 Robert Louis Stevenson, *Travels with a Donkey in the Cevennes* (1870), www.gutenberg.org.

20 Paul-Gerard Pasols, pp. 51–2.

21 Elizabeth Wilson, *Adorned in Dreams: Fashion and Modernity*. London: Virago Press, 1985, p. 154.

22 Johnson, p. 1.

23 Charlotte Perkins Gilman, *Herland* (1915), www.gutenberg.org.

24 Charlotte Perkins Gilman, *If I were a Man* (1914), www.gutenberg.org.

25 Alice Duer Miller, "Why We Oppose Pockets for Women!" (1915), www.gutenberg.org.

26 Loelia Ponsonby, *Grace and Favour: Memoirs of Loelia Duchess of Westminster*. London: Shenval Press, 1961, p. 450.

27 Cecil Beaton, *The Glass of Fashion*. London: Cassell, 1989, p. 3.

28 Lucile, Lady Duff Gordon, *Discretions and Indiscretions*. London: Jarrolds, 1932, pp. 107–8.

CULT OF THE CLUTCH

1 Quoted in Penny Sparke, *As Long As It's Pink: The Sexual Politics of Taste*. London: Pandora, 1995, p. 107.

2 Ibid., p. 73.

3 Adolf Loos, quoted in ibid., p. 106.

4 Adolf Loos, quoted in Elizabeth Wilson, *The Sphinx in the City*. London: Virago, 1991, p. 91.

5 Cecil Beaton, *The Glass of Fashion*. London: Cassell, 1989, p. 152.

6 Farid Chenoune, *Carried Away: All About Bags*. New York: The Vendome Press, 2005, p. 40.

7 Ibid.

8 Dorothy Parker, "Dust Before Fireworks," *The Best of Dorothy Parker*. London: The Folio Society, 1995, p. 73.

9 Loelia Ponsonby, *Grace and Favour: Memoirs of Loelia Duchess of Westminster*. London: Shenval Press, 1961, p. 108.

10 Beaton, pp. 152–3.

11 Quoted in Billie Melman, *Women and the Popular Imagination: Flapper and Nymphs*. London: Macmillan Press, 1988, p. 22.

12 Michael Arlen, *The Green Hat*. London: W. Collins and Co. Ltd., 1924, p. 16.

13 Virginia Woolf, quoted in Wilson, p. 157.

14 Katherine Mansfield, "The Escape," *Bliss and Other Stories*. New York: Alfred A. Knopf, 1920, p. 274.

15 Quoted in Robert Friedel, *Zipper: An Exploration in Novelty*. New York: W. W. Norton and Company, 1994, p. 212.

16 Ibid., pp. 16, 39.

17 Ibid., p. 174.

18 Aldous Huxley, *Brave New World* (1932), quoted in ibid., p. 211.

19 Nancy Mitford, *The Pursuit of Love*. London: The Folio Society, 1991, pp. 61–2.

20 Lynn Fontanne, quoted in Richard Corson, *Fashions in Hair: The First Five Thousand Years*. London: Peter Owen, 2001, p. 616.

21 Caroline Evans, "Masks, Mirrors and Mannequins: Elsa Schiaparelli and the Decentred Subject," *Fashion Theory*, Vol. 3, Issue 1, 1999, p. 19.

22 Kathy Peiss, *Hope in a Jar: The Making of America's Beauty Culture*. New York: Metropolitan Books, 1998, p. 155.

23 Zelda Fitzgerald, quoted in Colin McDowell, *The Literary Companion to Fashion*. London: Sinclair–Stevenson, 1995, p. 64.

24 Parker, "Cousin Larry," p. 206.

25 Anna Johnson, *Handbags: The Power of the Purse*. New York: Workman Publishing, 2002, p. 415.

26 Mary Ann Caws, *The Surrealist Look: An Erotics of Encounter*. Cambridge, Massachusetts: MIT Press, 1997, p. 4.

27 Quoted in Claire Wilcox, *Bags*. London: V&A Publications, 1999, p. 85.

28 Elsa Schiaparelli, *Shocking Life*. London: J.M. Dent and Sons, 1954, p. 150.

CARRYING COUTURE

1 Carol Shields, "A Purse of One's Own," *A Second Skin: Women Write About Clothes*, edited by Kirsty Dunseath. London: The Women's Press, 1998, p. 11.

2 Cecil Beaton, *The Glass of Fashion*. London: Cassell, 1989, p. 243.

3 Christina Stead, *A Little Tea, A Little Chat*. London: Virago, 1945, pp. 284–5.

4 Edna and Ilka Woolman Chase, *Always in Vogue*. London: Victor Gollancz Ltd., 1954, p. 190.

5 Betty Page, *On Fair Vanity*. London: Convoy Publications, 1954, p. 140.

6 Jean Dawnay, *Model Girl*. London: Weidenfeld and Nicolson, 1956, p. 140.

7 Anne Scott-James, *In the Mink*. London: Purnell and Sons, 1953, pp. 139, 140.

8 Christian Dior quoted in Valerie Steele and Laird Borelli, *Bags: A Lexicon of Style*. London: Scriptum Editions, 1999, p. 25.

9 Dawnay, p. 69.

10 Ginette Spanier, *It Isn't All Mink*. London: Collins, 1959, p. 192.

11 Ibid., pp. 178–9.

12 Berenice Geoffroy-Schneiter, *Bags*. Paris: Assouline, 2004, p. 16.

13 Inga Guen quoted in Annie Groer, "Hermes v. Hermes," *The Washington Post*, June 28, 2006.

14 Joyce McKinnell, *Blueprints for Beauty*. London: Collins, 1964, p. 22.

15 Dora Shackell, *Accent on Accessories* (1957), quoted in Claire Wilcox, *Bags*. London: V&A Publications, 1999, p. 99.

16 Eileen McCarthy, *Frankly Feminine*. London: The Grolier Society, 1965, p. 87.

17 McKinnell, p. 19.

18 Ibid., p. 95.

19 Constance Moore, *The Way to Beauty*. London: Ward, Lock and Co., 1955, p. 73.

20 McCarthy, p. 89.

21 Spanier, p. 86.

22 Page, p. 19.

23 Emily Kimbrough, *Forty Plus and Fancy Free*. London: Constable, 1955, pp. 108–9.

24 Shields, p. 14.

25 St. John Irvine, "Have Girls too much Freedom?" *Homes and Gardens*, June, 1956, pp. 44–5.

26 Penny Sparke, *As Long As It's Pink: The Sexual Politics of Taste*. London: Pandora, 1995, p. 188.

27 Marnie Fogg, interview with the author, 2006.

28 Roland Barthes, *Mythologies*. London: Paladin, 1973, p. 98.

29 Edward Adler, *Living It Up*. New York: Ace Books, 1955, pp. 6–7.

30 Mary Elizabeth Williams, *Bagging the Big One: The Plastic Purse*. www.stim.com.

31 "Lucite Handbags: A Guide to Plastic Purses of the 1950s." www.memberstripod.com.

32 Sara Cameron, "Plastic Handbags: Then and Now." www.scarletdukes.com.

33 Lawrence Langner, *The Importance of Wearing Clothes*. London: Constable, 1959, pp. 325–6.

FAST TO THE FUTURE

1 Elizabeth Wilson and Lou Taylor, *Through the Looking Glass: A History of Dress from 1860 to the Present Day*. London: BBC Books, 1989, p. 169.

2 Georgina Howell, *In Vogue: Sixty Years of Celebrities and Fashion from British Vogue*. London: Penguin, 1978, p. 278.

3 Kenneth Leech, *Youthquake*. London: Sheldon Press, 1973.

4 John Corsby, quoted in Howell, p. 253.

5 Marnie Fogg, *Boutique*. London: Mitchell Beazley, 2003, p. 8.

6 Colin MacInnes, *Absolute Beginners* (1959). London: Allison and Busby, 1980, p. 32.

7 Mary Quant, *Quant by Quant* (1965). London: Pan, 1967, p. 48.

8 Mary Quant, quoted in Valerie Steele, *Fifty Years of Fashion: New Look to Now*. New Haven: Yale University Press, 1997, p. 51.

9 Quant, pp. 87–8.

10 Ibid., pp. 80–8.

11 Twiggy, quoted in Fogg, p. 22.

12 Janet Street-Porter, *Baggage, My Childhood*. London: Headline, 2004, p. 185.

13 Marnie Fogg, interview with the author, 2006.

14 Valerie Thurlow, *Model in Paris*, London: Robert Hale, 1975, p. 34.

15 Twiggy, *Twiggy: An Autobiography*. London: Hart-Davis, MacGibbon Ltd., 1975, p. 14.

16 Fogg, 2006.

17 Claire Wilcox, *Bags*. London: V&A Publications, 1999, p. 104.

18 Sylvia Plath, quoted in Judith Watt, *The Penguin Book of Twentieth Century Fashion Writing*. London: Penguin, 2000, p. 265.

19 Thurlow, p. 40.

20 Richard Morais, *Pierre Cardin: The Man Who Became a Label*. London: Bantam Press, 1991, p. 111.

21 Ibid., p. 112.

22 Andy Warhol, quoted in Wilson and Taylor, p. 177.

23 Andy Warhol, quoted in Watt, p. 271.

24 Jennifer Harris, Sarah Hyde, and Greg Smith, *1966 and All That: Design and the Consumer in Britain 1960–1969*. London: Trefoil Design Library, 1986, p. 25.

25 Bonnie Cashin, quoted in Anna Johnson, *Handbags: The Power of the Purse*. New York: Workman Publishing, 2002, p. 385.

26 Andy Warhol, quoted in Richard Martin, editor, *Contemporary Fashion*, London: St James' Press, 1995, p. 150.

27 Germaine Greer, "1968 and All That," *Independent on Sunday*, February 8, 1998, p. 12.

28 Simon Cooper, *The Rag Dolls*. London: Souvenir Press, 1968, p. 297.

29 Martin, p. 150.

30 Rudi Gernreich, quoted in Andrew Bolton, *Men in Skirts*. London: V&A Publications, 2003, p. 21.

31 Farid Chenoune, *A History of Men's Fashion*. New York: Flammarion, 1993, p. 248.

32 Truman Capote, quoted in Valerie Steele and Laird Borelli, *Bags: A Lexicon of Style*. London: Scriptum Editions, 1999, p. 176.

33 Marnie Fogg, interview with the author 2006.

34 Ibid.

35 Wilson and Taylor, p. 171.

36 http://homepage.ntlworld.com/carousel/pob07.html.

LOGO-MANIA

1 Diana Vreeland, quoted in Debora Silverman, *Selling Culture: Bloomingdale's, Diana Vreeland, and the New Aristocracy of Taste in Reagan's America*. New York: Pantheon Books, 1986, p 3

2 Richard Neville, *Playpower*. London: Paladin, 1970, p. 74.

3 Germaine Greer, *The Female Eunuch*. London: Paladin, 1971, p. 55.

4 Richard Morais, *Pierre Cardin: The Man Who Became a Label*. London: Bantam Press, 1991, p. 112.

5 Susan Brownmiller, *Femininity*. London: Hamish Hamilton, 1984, p. 199.

6 Roger Saul, quoted in Richard Martin, editor, *Contemporary Fashion*. London: St James' Press, 1995, p. 380.

7 Abigail Healey, interview with the author, 2006.

8 Mark Jacobson, "Disco Dreams" (1975), quoted in Peter Knobler and Greg Mitchell, editors, *Very Seventies: A Cultural History of the 1970s, from the pages of Crawdaddy*. New York: Fireside, 1995, p. 114.

9 Carlos Falchi, quoted in Anna Johnson, *Handbags: The Power of the Purse*. New York: Workman Publishing, 2002, pp. 234–5.

10 www.fashion-and-style.org.

11 Georgina Howell, *In Vogue: Sixty Years of Celebrities and Fashion from British Vogue*. London: Penguin, 1978, p. 306.

12 Mark Tungate, *Fashion Brands: Branding Style from Armani to Zara*. London: Kogan Page, 2005, p. 15.

13 Ibid.

14 Quoted in Morais, p. 143.

15 Daniel Boorstein, quoted in ibid., p. 181.

16 Brett Easton Ellis, *American Psycho*. New York: Vintage Books, 1991, pp. 41–3.

17 Ibid., p. 241.

18 Ibid., pp. 241–2.

19 Pearson Phillips, *Yaps: The Complete Guide to Young Aspiring Professionals*. London: Arrow Books, 1984, pp. 15–16.

20 Ibid.

21 John T. Molloy, *Women, Dress For Success*. London: W. Foulsham and Co. Ltd., 1980, p. 18.

22 Ibid., p. 174.

23 Ibid., p. 93.

24 Wendy Webster, *Not a Man to Match Her: The Marketing of a Prime Minister*. London: The Women's Press, 1990, p. 56.

25 Quoted in ibid., p. 80.

26 Tom Wolfe, *The Bonfire of the Vanities*. London: Jonathan Cape, 1988, pp. 86–7.

27 Johnson, pp. 100–1.

28 Silverman, p. 5.

29 Wolfe, pp. 373–4.

30 Carlo Celoni, quoted in Kitty Kelley, *Nancy Reagan: The Unauthorised Biography*. London: Transworld Publishers, 1991, p. 255.

31 Ibid., p. 321.

32 Irving Layton, *The Gucci Bag*. Oakville, Ontario: Mosaic Press, 1984, p. 16.

33 Ibid., p. 19.

ARM CANDY

1 Quoted in Marie Browning, *Purse Pizzazz*. New York: Stirling Publishing Co., 2005, p. 9.

2 Quoted in Richard Martin, editor, *Contemporary Fashion*, London: St James' Press, 1995, p. 421.

3 Lisa Armstrong, "The New Snobbery," *Vogue*, April 1995, p. 172.

4 William Langley, "Farewell to High Fashion?" (London) *Evening Standard*, January 22, 1993, quoted in Rebecca Arnold, *Fashion, Desire and Anxiety: Image and Morality in the 20th Century*. London: I. B. Tauris, 2001, p. 11.

5 www.karrysafe.com.

6 Ibid.

7 Valerie Steele and Laird Borelli, *Bags: A Lexicon of Style*. London: Scriptum Editions, 1999, pp. 170–3.

8 Quoted in ibid., p. 173.

9 Karl Lagerfeld, quoted in Elsa Klensch, "Bag It! Chanel, Prada Accessories for Fall," September 18, 1998, www.cnn.com/STYLE/9809/18/prada.chanel.

10 Nathalie Hambro, quoted in Charlotte Skene-Catling, *Nathalie Hambro: The Art of the Handbag*. London: NMH, 1999, p. 8.

11 Nathalie Hambro, quoted in Steele and Borelli, pp. 140, 149.

12 Lauren Weisberger, *The Devil Wears Prada*. London: Harper Collins, 2003, p. 182.

13 Mimi Spencer, quoted in Steele and Borelli, p. 10.

14 Zoe Williams, "To Them, Free. To You, £595," *The Guardian*, May 31, 2006, http://www.guardian.co.uk/Columnists/Column/0,,1786373,00.htm.l.

15 Alice Fisher, "£2,250 for a Handbag?" *Observer Magazine*, July 23, 2006, p. 33.

16 Quoted in ibid.

17 Imogen Edwards-Jones, *Fashion Babylon*. London: Bantam Press, 2006, p. 98.

18 Bryan Appleyard, "Want Taste Today? Get Bags of Money," *Sunday Times Culture* (London), January 29, 2006, p. 9.

19 Ibid., p. 9.

20 Stuart Vevers, quoted in Claudia Croft, "Gotta Have It," *Sunday Times Style* (London), July 17, 2005, p. 26.

21 Lulu Guinness, quoted in Elizabeth A. Kennedy, "A Brand New Bag," http://www.flatrock.org.nz/topics/lifestyles/whats_in_a_handbag.htm.

22 Jan Birks, interview with the author, 2006.

23 Patrick Barkham, "Papa's got a brand new bag," *The Guardian*, June 29, 2006, http://www.guardian.co.uk/g2/story/0,,1808518,00.html.

24 "Passnotes No. 204: Manbags," *The Times* (London), June 29, 2006, p. 2.

BIBLIOGRAPHY

Adler, Edward, *Living It Up*. New York: Ace Books, 1955.

Akass, Kim and McCabe, Janet (editors), *Reading Sex and the City*. London: I. B. Tauris, 2004.

Allen, Carmel, *The Handbag: To Have and to Hold*. London: Carlton Books, 1999.

Appleyard, Bryan, "Want Taste Today? Get Bags of Money," *Sunday Times Culture* (London), January 29, 2006, p. 9.

Arlen, Michael, *The Green Hat*. London: W. Collins and Co. Ltd., 1924.

Armstrong, Lisa, "The New Snobbery," *Vogue*, April 1995.

Arnold, Rebecca, *Fashion, Desire and Anxiety: Image and Morality in the 20th Century*. London: I. B. Tauris, 2001.

Barkham, Patrick, "Papa's got a brand new bag," *The Guardian*, June 29, 2006.

Barthes, Roland, *Mythologies*. London: Paladin, 1973.

Battersby, Martin, *The Decorative Thirties*. London: Studio Vista, 1971.

Beaton, Cecil, *The Glass of Fashion*. London: Cassell, 1989.

Beckett, Jane and Cherry, Deborah (editors), *The Edwardian Era*. London: Barbican Art Gallery, 1987.

Bell, Quentin, *On Human Finery*. London: Allison and Busby, 1992.

Bowd, Emma, *A Passion for Handbags*. London: Ryland, Peters and Small, 2002.

Bolton, Andrew, *Men in Skirts*. London: V&A Publications, 2003.

Browning, Marie, *Purse Pizzazz*. New York: Sterling Publishing Co., 2005.

Brownmiller, Susan, *Femininity*. London: Hamish Hamilton, 1984.

Brush-Kidwell, Claudia and Steele, Valerie (editors), *Men and Women: Dressing the Part*. Washington: Smithsonian Institution Press, 1989.

Cameron, Sarah, "Plastic Handbags: Then and Now," www.scarletdukes.com.

Caws, Mary Ann, *The Surrealist Look: An Erotics of Encounter*. Cambridge, Massachusetts: MIT Press, 1997.

Chenoune, Farid, *A History of Men's Fashion*. New York: Flammarion, 1993.

— *Carried Away: All About Bags*. New York: The Vendome Press, 2005.

Cooper, Simon, *The Rag Dolls*. London: Souvenir Press, 1968.

Corson, Richard, *Fashions in Hair: The First Five Thousand Years*. London: Peter Owen, 2001.

Croft, Claudia, "Gotta Have It," *Sunday Times Style* (London), July 17, 2005.

Cunnington, C. W. and P., *Handbook of English Costume in the Eighteenth Century*. London: Faber and Faber, 1972.

Davidoff, Leonore and Hall, Catherine, *Family Fortunes: Men and Women of the English Middle Class 1780–1850*. London: Routledge, 1997.

Davidson, E., *The Bag*. Leeds City Council, Department of Education, Community Education Service, 1978.

Dawnay, Jean, *Model Girl*. London: Weidenfeld and Nicolson, 1956.

Dunseath, Kirsty (editor), *A Second Skin: Women Write About Clothes*. London: The Women's Press, 1998.

Easton Ellis, Brett, *American Psycho*. New York: Vintage Books, 1991.

Edwards-Jones, Imogen, *Fashion Babylon*. London: Bantam Press, 2006.

Ericson, Lois, *The Bag Book*. London: Van Nostrand Reinhold, 1976.

Evans, Caroline, "Masks, Mirrors and Mannequins: Elsa Schiaparelli and the Decentred Subject," *Fashion Theory*, Vol. 3, Issue 1.

Fisher, Alice, "£2,250 for a Handbag?" *Observer Magazine*, July 23, 2006.

Fitzgerald, F. Scott, *The Diamond as Big as the Ritz and Other Stories*. London: Penguin, 1962.

Fogg, Marnie, *Boutique*. London: Mitchell-Beazley, 2003.

Foster, Hal, *Compulsive Beauty*. Cambridge, Massachusetts: MIT Press, 1995.

Foster, Vanda, *Bags and Purses*. London: Batsford, 1982.

Friedel, Robert, *Zipper: An Exploration in Novelty*. New York: W. W. Norton and Company, 1994.

Gaskin, Sarah, *Everything but the Kitchen Sink? The Material Culture of Victorian Women's Travel c. 1840–c. 1900*. Unpublished Dissertation. V&A/RCA History of Design, 2002.

Geoffroy-Schneiter, Berenice, *Bags*. Paris: Assouline, 2004.

Gilman, Perkins Charlotte, *If I were a Man* (1914), www.gutenberg.org.

— *Herland* (1915), www.gutenberg.org.

Greer, Germaine, *The Female Eunuch*. London: Paladin, 1971.

— "1968 and All That," *Independent on Sunday*, February 8, 1998.

Groer, Annie, "Hermes v. Hermes," *Washington Post*, June 28, 2006.

Hansen, Joseph and Reed, Evelyn, *Cosmetics, Fashions and the Exploitation of Women*. London: Pathfinder Press, 1986.

Hardy, Lady Violet, *As It Was*. London: Christopher Johnson, 1958.

Harris, Jennifer, Hyde, Sarah, and Smith, Greg, *1966 and All That: Design and the Consumer in Britain 1960–1969*. London: Trefoil Design Library, 1986.

Hendrikje Bag Museum, *Bags*. Amsterdam: The Pepin Press, 2004.

Hillier, Bevis, *The Style of the Century*. London: The Herbert Press, 1998.

Howell, Georgina, *In Vogue*. London: Penguin Books, 1975.

Humphrey, John T., "Useful Bags and How to Make Them," *Scientific American Supplement*, No. 561, October 2, 1886.

Irvine, St. John, "Have Girls Too Much Freedom?" *Homes and Gardens*, June, 1956, pp. 44–45.

Jacobson, Mark, "Disco Dreams" (1975), in Peter Knobler and Greg Mitchell (editors), *Very Seventies: A Cultural History of the 1970s, from the pages of Crawdaddy*. New York: Fireside, 1995.

Johnson, Anna, *Handbags: The Power of the Purse*. New York: Workman Publishing, 2002.

Kaplan, Louise J., *Female Perversions*. London: Penguin, 1999.

Kelley, Kitty, *Nancy Reagan: The Unauthorised Biography*. London: Transworld Publishers, 1991.

Kirkham, Pat (editor), *The Gendered Object*. Manchester: Manchester University Press, 1996.

Kimbrough, Emily, *Forty Plus and Fancy Free*. Constable, London, 1955.

Klensch, Elsa, *Bag It! Chanel, Prada Accessories for Fall*, www.cnn.com.

Langner, Lawrence, *The Importance of Wearing Clothes*. London: Constable, 1959.

Laver, James, *Taste and Fashion*. London: George G. Harrap and Company, 1937.

Layton, Irving, *The Gucci Bag*. London: Mosaic, 1984.

Leech, Kenneth, *Youthquake*. London: Sheldon Press, 1973.

Lewis, Peter, *The Fifties*. London: Heinemann, 1978.

Lucile, Lady Duff Gordon, *Discretions and Indiscretions*. London: Jarrolds, 1932.

"Lucite Handbags: A Guide to Plastic Purses of the 1950s," www.memberstripod.com.

Lurie, Alison, *The Language of Clothes*. London: Hamlyn, 1983.

MacInnes, Colin, *Absolute Beginners* (1959), London: Allison and Busby, 1980.

Mansfield, Katherine, "The Escape," *Bliss and Other Stories*. New York: Alfred A. Knopf, 1920.

Martin, Richard, *Fashion and Surrealism*. New York: Rizzoli, 1987.

Martin, Richard (editor), *Contemporary Fashion*. London: St James Press, 1995.

McCarthy, Eileen, *Frankly Feminine*. London: The Grolier Society, 1965.

McDermott, Catherine, *Made in Britain: Tradition and Style in Contemporary British Fashion*. London: Mitchell-Beazley, 2002.

McDowell, Colin, *The Literary Companion to Fashion*. London: Sinclair-Stevenson, 1995.

McKinnell, Joyce, *Blueprints for Beauty*. London: Collins, 1964.

Melman, Billie, *Women and the Popular Imagination: Flapper and Nymphs*. London: Macmillan Press, 1988.

Miller, Alice Duer, "Why We Oppose Pockets for Women!" (1915), www.gutenberg.org.

Miller, Judith, *Handbags*. London: Dorling Kindersley, 2006.

Mitford, Nancy, *The Pursuit of Love*. London: The Folio Society, 1991.

Molloy, John T., *Women, Dress for Success*. London: W. Foulsham and Co. Ltd., 1980.

Moore, Constance, *The Way to Beauty*. London: Ward, Lock and Co., 1955.

Morais, Richard, *Pierre Cardin: The Man Who Became a Label*. London: Bantam Press, 1991.

Neville, Richard, *Playpower*. London: Paladin, 1970.

Page, Betty, *On Fair Vanity*. London: Convoy Publications, 1954.

Parker, Dorothy, *The Best of Dorothy Parker*. London: The Folio Society, 1995.

Pasols, Paul-Gerard, *Louis Vuitton: The Birth of Modern Luxury*. New York: Harry N. Abrams, 2005.

"Passnotes No. 204: Manbags," *The Times* (London), June 29, 2006, p. 2.

Peiss, Kathy, *Hope in a Jar: The Making of America's Beauty Culture*. New York: Metropolitan Books, 1998.

Philips, Pearson, *Yaps: The Complete Guide to Young Aspiring Professionals*. London: Arrow Books, 1984.

Ponsonby, Loelia, *Grace and Favour: Memoirs of Loelia Duchess of Westminster*. London: Shenval Press, 1961.

Quant, Mary, *Quant by Quant* (1965), London: Pan, 1967.

Rawsthorn, Alice, *Yves Saint Laurent*. London: Harper Collins, 1996.

Ribeiro, Aileen, *Dress and Morality*. New York: Holmes and Meier, 1986.

— *Dress in Eighteenth Century Europe 1715–1789*. New Haven and London: Yale University Press, 2002.

Schiaparelli, Elsa, *Shocking Life*. London: J. M. Dent and Sons, 1954.

Scott-James, Anne, *In the Mink*. London: Purnell and Sons, 1953.

Singer, Ruth and Barrett, Gina, *Medieval Textile Purses*. London: Soper Lane, 2004.

Silverman, Debora, *Selling Culture: Bloomingdale's, Diana Vreeland, and the New Aristocracy of Taste in Reagan's America*. New York: Pantheon Books, 1986.

Skene-Catling, Charlotte, *Nathalie Hambro: The Art of the Handbag*. London: NMH, 1999.

Skramsrad, Harold K. Jr., *Streamlining America*. Michigan: Henry Ford Museum and Greenfield Village, 1987.

Sparke, Penny, *As Long As It's Pink: The Sexual Politics of Taste*. London: Pandora, 1995.

Spanier, Ginette, *It Isn't All Mink*. London: Collins, 1959.

Stead, Christina, *A Little Tea, A Little Chat*. London: Virago, 1945.

Steele, Valerie, *Paris Fashion: A Cultural History*. Oxford: Oxford University Press, 1988.

— *Fifty Years of Fashion: New Look to Now*. New Haven: Yale University Press, 1997.

— and Borelli, Laird, *Bags: A Lexicon of Style*. London: Scriptum Editions, 1999.

Street-Porter, Janet, *Baggage*. London: Headline Book Publishing, 2004.

Stevenson, Robert Louis, *Travels with a Donkey in the Cevennes* (1870), www.gutenberg.org.

Thurlow, Valerie, *Model in Paris*. London: Robert Hale and Co., 1975.

Tolstoy, Leo, *Anna Karenina*, 1875, www.literature.org.

Trefusis, Violet, *Hunt the Slipper* (1937). London: Virago, 1983.

Tungate, Mark, *Fashion Brands: Branding Style from Armani to Zara*. London: Kogan Page, 2005.

Twiggy, *Twiggy: An Autobiography*. London: Hart-Davis, MacGibbon Ltd., 1975.

Watt, Judith, *The Penguin Book of Twentieth Century Fashion Writing*. London: Penguin, 2000.

Webster, Wendy, *Not a Man to Match Her: The Marketing of a Prime Minister*. London: The Women's Press, 1990.

Weisberger, Lauren, *The Devil Wears Prada*. London: Harper Collins, 2003.

The Williamsburg Garden Club, *A Williamsburg Scrapbook*. Richmond, Virginia: The Dietz Printing Co., 1937.

Wilcox, Claire, *Bags*. London: V&A Publications, 1999.

Williams, Beryl, *Fashion is Our Business*. London: John Gifford Limited, 1948.

Williams, Mary Elizabeth, "Bagging the Big One: the Plastic Purse," www.stim.com.

Williams, Zoe, "To Them, Free. To You, £595," *The Guardian*, May 31, 2006.

Wilson, Elizabeth, *Adorned in Dreams: Fashion and Modernity*. London: Virago Press, 1985.

— *The Sphinx in the City: Urban Life, the Control of Disorder, and Women*. London: Virago, 1991.

— and Taylor, Lou, *Through the Looking Glass: A History of Dress from 1860 to the Present Day*. London: BBC Books, 1989.

Wolfe, Tom, *The Bonfire of the Vanities*. London: Jonathan Cape, 1988.

Woolman Chase, Edna and Ilka, *Always in Vogue*. London: Victor Gollancz Ltd., 1954.

Zdatny, Steven, "The Boyish Look and the Liberated Woman: The Politics and Aesthetics of Women's Hairstyles," *Fashion Theory*, Vol. 1, Issue 4, 1997.

PICTURE CREDITS

INDEX